HARLEM REALLY COOKS

by SANDRA LAWRENCE

ILLUSTRATIONS *by* BENNY ANDREWS

lake isle press

Published by:
Lake Isle Press, Inc.
16 West 32nd Street, Suite 10-B
New York, NY 10001
(212) 273-0796
E-mail: lakeisle@earthlink.net

Distributed to the trade by:
National Book Network, Inc.
4501 Forbes Boulevard, Suite 200
Lanham, MD 20706
1(800) 462-6420
www.nbnbooks.com

Library of Congress Control Number: 2006930193

ISBN-13: 978-1-891105-18-0

ISBN-10: 1-891105-18-3

Complete list of illustration credits: see page 192

Book and cover design: Ellen Swandiak

Editors: Pimpila Thanaporn and Katherine Trimble

First edition

Printed in the United States of America

10 9 8 7 6 5 4 3 2 1

DEDICATION

To my mother, Lossie "Doll" Lawrence, who was the inspiration for this book, and the best cook ever!

ACKNOWLEDGMENTS

Dorothy Vaughn is the most supportive friend anyone ever had. I have been blessed with her loving care and loyalty. It is because of her faith in me and her encouragement that this book has finally been completed. I had become discouraged when for years prospects were looking dim. My friend Dot believed in me and in the value of this book. She pushed me forward and told me to keep working on it and to keep trying to get others interested in it. I give thanks for her being in my life.

Hiroko Kiiffner and Lake Isle Press have helped me to fulfill my dream. Hiroko's vision allowed her to "see" and believe in the final product; *Harlem Really Cooks*. She made it happen.

I especially thank my family and friends for their love and support. Katherine Lyles, my cousin, put the text on disk when I needed it done "immediately," a skill that I did not possess. Irene Vargas helped with knowledge that she acquired at the New School University on "how to organize a cookbook." Christina Colon and Paul Evans, Jr. were my "tasters" and expert consultants. Yesie often graced my table with exotic Ethiopian dishes.

I would like to give a special acknowledgment to my friends at the Senegalese Bakery at 143rd Street and Amsterdam Avenue.

There are many more, some of whom are mentioned in the recipes included here, others who gave me general moral support and touched my life in ways they will never know. To all of you I want to say "thank you so much."

A NOTE FROM THE ARTIST

My first thoughts of art for a cookbook were still life images of food, reminiscent of paintings done by artists over the years. Hanging pheasants, glowing fruits, and elegant serving platters came to mind. However, when I started to read the recipes in this book, many of dishes I'd grown up loving, I began to remember also the people, places, and events to which these foods are so closely tied.

There were so many special occasions where food was central to what was happening. Sunday church dinners spread out on benches on the grounds, each family with offerings of their favorite dishes–meats, vegetables, cakes, and pies. We, the children, ran from one dessert to another while the minister was being fed by the sisters, and the deacons ate and discussed farm work at the same time.

And so it was easy for me to forgo the still life portraits of food, choosing instead to show some of the doings of the people who cooked, ate, and enjoyed these wonderful, traditional dishes, in this case, up north in Harlem.

–Benny Andrews

FOREWORD

Sandra's life was steeped in her African Heritage and nurtured in the place she lovingly called home from birth 'til death–HARLEM. She loved Harlem's history, its rhythms, its soul, but most of all its unique infusion of southern, Caribbean, African, and Spanish cuisines. She felt that much of Harlem's history had been well documented, but that no one had collected, in one volume, the varied cultural dishes that were prepared and enjoyed by Harlem families, friends, and fellow gourmands. Thus *Harlem Really Cooks* was born.

She traveled extensively throughout Africa and Europe enjoying the art and cuisines of both continents but she always had a deep-seated desire to introduce and expose the Nouvelle Soul Food of Harlem which she prepared, shared, and enjoyed for a lifetime.

As her friend of 40 years, I am proud of Sandra's tenacity and determination in staying the course to see that this personal and often intimate piece of Harlem's Soul would not be forgotten. She will not be, either.

–Dorothy Bruce Vaughn

COTTON CLUB

INTRODUCTION

Harlem has always tantalized visitors with its rhythm, vitality, and creativity. A New York tourist mecca, it boasts splendid architecture, landmarks, churches, museums, and dance companies. But the greatest way to experience Harlem today is through dining, whether it be in a neighborhood restaurant, or at home. The varied cultures of the community are expressed in traditional dishes, as well as a fusion of all. The predominant fare is soul food, which evolved from the inventive ways in which our ancestors made do with limited provisions during slavery. The ancestors who made it through the middle passage had prepared for their horrific journey with seeds of okra, yam, and black-eyed peas. This, with provisions of lesser cuts of pork, corn, and plantation grown vegetables, became a source of survival. To this extent I honor this food, and celebrate the creative ways in which it was prepared then, as well as the exciting, more complex ways in which it can be prepared today. So skilled were these early cooks, that their influence was felt all over the South, forming the basis of what is known as Southern cooking.

Harlem was established in 1658 by the Dutch Governor Peter Stuyvesant and named after the Dutch city of Haarlem. The area was inhabited by the Dutch, followed by the British. During this time there were farms and large estates. But by 1830, the farms were no longer flourishing. The economy could not support the upkeep of these grand estates, and they were sold. The advent of elevated rail lines, constructed between 1837 and 1886, transformed this rural area into a middle and upper class neighborhood. On the West side, luxury apartment buildings rose, as well as brick town houses, which have contributed to Harlem's allure ever since. As the area was being redefined as a community, churches and schools were also built. As a result, Harlem has some of the most beautiful churches in the city, churches that are the bedrock of the community today.

Real estate speculation between 1898 and 1904 led to overbuilding, which resulted in vacancies, and foreclosed mortgages. To protect their investments, landlords lowered their rents. Philip Payton, a Black real estate broker, saw this as a chance to market the area to his people, which had not been possible in the past. At this time, there were many African Americans who had been successful in small businesses, and they made the move North. One of the largest influxes came with the construction of Pennsylvania Station between 1906 and 1910, which displaced Black residents in the area. Harlem was now established as an African American community.

By 1920, Blacks were migrating from the South and the West Indies. Harlem was the place to be. The community had become legendary, a place where self-expression was exploding with creativity. Writers, poets, fine artists, musicians, photographers, and trendsetters all lived and created together, and were inspired by each other's talents. These were the best of times: the Harlem Renaissance. This was the time of Zora Neale Hurston, Langston Hughes, Augusta Savage, James Weldon Johnson, Alain Locke, and W.E.B. DuBois. Duke Ellington, who gave America its own classical music, Lena Horn, Louis Armstrong, and others all made an enduring impression on music. White patrons of the arts found their way uptown, as did white bon vivants who needed a place to play. Harlem was cooking.

The depression saw the end of the Harlem Renaissance. The early 1930s found Harlemites jobless, but also demanding social change. White-owned stores refused to hire Blacks, and this led to the riot of 1935. Harlem found a strong political leader in Adam Clayton Powell, Jr., a young pastor at the Abyssinian Baptist Church who organized and led protest demonstrations. This was the beginning of Reverend Powell's career as an activist, a path that would lead him to a seat in Congress. The Great Depression ended with the beginning of World War II. Harlem was at the height of its jazz age, and the world took note of what was happening here in the jazz clubs.

Urban decay blighted the community during the '50s and by the early part of the '60s, the middle class began an exodus to Queens and Westchester. Despite the reservations of some regarding the mood of Harlem, it was still the place to be. Count Basie's, The Zambezi, Minton's, The Lenox Lounge, The Savoy, and Wells. This is where you went after dinner at The Red Rooster or Jock's, with their private club-like atmosphere. This is where you rubbed shoulders with professionals and drank champagne with your chitterlings. Obie's was where you went for breakfast. Most of these clubs and restaurants are now closed, but like the music, the memory lingers on.

Not much changed in the '70s, but the '80s saw a new dawn. The children of those who had moved to the suburbs were moving back. The allure of buildings with fine architectural integrity, two universities, the best transportation in the city, bucolic parks, boulevards, and tree-lined streets had once again become the setting for art galleries, ethnic shops, and dance companies.

Harlem's historic districts, designated by the city's Landmarks Preservation Commission, have created interest in the area from around the world. From the early '90s on, busloads of tourists have come to visit these sites and experience the vibrancy of its neighborhoods. New row houses are being built, grand old buildings are being renovated, and brownstoners are restoring their treasured houses.

Today, soul food is considered to be the traditional food of Black people, and it is cooked in much the same way. Harlem, however, has become more contemporary, with its diverse community of Blacks from the South, the Caribbean, and Africa, Latinos from Central and South America, as well as a growing number of American and European whites.

We Harlemites travel internationally, dine at a plethora of international restaurants in the city, and share the varied cuisines of our neighbors. We have become quite adept at reinventing some of our recipes, with a little bit of something new, but never losing the basics of classic soul food. We do our ancestors proud, that we have taken their recipes and added a splash of wine, a pinch of cumin, some virgin olive oil, a clove of garlic, unlimited heat and soul in our Cuisinart pot, just cooking away on the Garland. Harlem really cooks.

WINTER

SPRING

SUMMER

AUTUMN

WINTER

NEW YEAR'S DAY MENU

•

CUBAN ROAST PORK
WITH LIME

HOPPIN' JOHN
(BLACK-EYED PEAS)
WITH RICE

MIXED GREENS

SWEET POTATO PIE

suggessted drink:
POMMERY BRUT ROSÉ
CHAMPAGNE NV

see recipes page 46

winter

I GOT THE BLUES COMFORT POT

“The blues hang around every corner, on every stoop, and up and down the streets and boulevards of Harlem. You hear it in the music. Comfort does come. Sometimes it is just being able to share a meal of something that reminds you of home, someone caring, something warm—something that really fills the void and the yearning for a better tomorrow. But it's no sin to eat this dish when you're feeling good either. . .”

menu

•

HAM HOCKS, STRING BEANS
& POTATOES

•

AVOCADO SALAD

•

CORNBREAD

•

BRANDIED APPLES

•

suggested drink:
ROSÉ WINE

•

serves 4

HAM HOCKS, STRING BEANS, AND POTATOES

4 large smoked ham hocks (pigs' knuckles)

3 cloves garlic, minced

2 bay leaves

1 tablespoon salt

1 tablespoon freshly ground black pepper

1 tablespoon onion powder

1 teaspoon crushed red pepper flakes

2 pounds string beans, trimmed

4 russet potatoes, halved

Rinse the ham hocks, place them in a 6-quart pot, and cover with water to 3 inches above the hocks. Add the garlic, bay leaves, salt, pepper, onion powder, and red pepper flakes. Bring the water to a boil, lower to a simmer, and cover. Simmer until the ham hock is soft and the skin is just about to burst, 3 to 3+1/2 hours. Add the string beans and potatoes and cook until the potatoes and beans are done, about 30 minutes.

Note: Choose ham hocks with a light tan color. The darker the hocks, the heavier the smoke; the darker ones will tend to be harder, too. Look for a good plug of ham on the wide end. Serves 4.

AVOCADO SALAD

In Africa and the Caribbean the avocado is called "pear." Both the purplish-black Hass and the green Fuerte avocados are good, and lend themselves well to salads, salad dressings, and of course, guacamole.

1 head red-leaf lettuce, washed and spun dry

3 large, ripe, green avocados or 5 to 6 small, ripe Hass avocados

1 large lemon, cut into wedges

Separate leaves from head of lettuce and arrange on salad plates. Pit and peel the avocados, cut them into wedges, and arrange on the lettuce leaves. Garnish each plate with a lemon wedge, and serve immediately. You can also squeeze lemon juice on the avocado before serving, to prevent them from discoloring. Serves 6.

CORNBREAD

Vegetable oil or butter, for pan

1 cup all-purpose flour, sifted

2 tablespoons sugar

2 tablespoons baking powder

1/2 teaspoon baking soda

1/2 teaspoon salt

1 cup yellow cornmeal

2 large eggs, beaten

1/4 cup (1/2 stick) unsalted butter, melted

1 cup milk

Preheat the oven to 425°. Grease an 8-inch square baking pan with vegetable oil or butter. In a medium bowl, sift together the flour, sugar, baking powder, baking soda, and salt. Add the cornmeal and combine. In a large bowl, mix the eggs, butter, and milk. Fold the flour mixture into the egg mixture and mix until smooth and moist. Do not over-mix. Pour the batter into the prepared pan, smoothing out to the edges of the pan. Bake until golden brown, 20 to 25 minutes. Cut the bread into squares. Serves 4 to 6.

BRANDIED APPLES

2 tablespoons butter

3 Granny Smith apples, cored, seeded, and cut into wedges

1/2 cup brandy

1 heaping tablespoon brown sugar

1/4 teaspoon cinnamon

Whipped cream, for serving

In a medium skillet over medium-low heat, melt the butter. Add the apples and sauté 4 minutes. Sprinkle with brandy, sugar, and cinnamon, and cook for 3 minutes. Spoon the apples into four individual dessert dishes, leaving the sauce in the pan. Increase the heat to medium-high and cook 1 minute to reduce the sauce. Spoon some sauce over each dish, top with whipped cream, and serve. Serves 4.

winter

SATURDAY AT DOLL'S HOUSE

"If you took the A train to Sugar Hill, you were sure to get what the Diva of Soul Food, my mother Doll, had been cooking since early morning. While she swept and dusted the house, those pots simmered away for hours, filling the air with the aromas that gave you a sense of security—you knew just how much love she put into that meal."

NOTE:
This entire menu can be prepared a day ahead.

menu

•

GLORIFIED TROTTERS
(PIGS' FEET)

•

COLLARD GREENS

•

POTATO SALAD DOLL'S WAY

•

GRANDMOTHER MINNIE'S
LEMON MERINGUE PIE

•

suggested drink:
CHAMPAGNE-POMMERY
BRUT ROYAL CHAMPAGNE NV

•

serves 4

GLORIFIED TROTTERS (PIGS' FEET)

8 pigs' feet, split in half

4 stalks celery

3 onions, peeled and quartered

1 (8-ounce) can tomato sauce

1/2 cup dry sherry

2 tablespoons salt

1 teaspoon crushed red pepper flakes

1 teaspoon freshly ground black pepper

2 bay leaves

2 cloves garlic

Apple cider vinegar, for serving

Hot sauce, such as Tabasco, for serving

Scrub the pigs' feet, and carefully singe off any hair with a lighter or a match. Put the pigs' feet in a 6-quart pot with the celery, onions, tomato sauce, sherry, salt, red pepper flakes, pepper, bay leaves, and garlic and cover with cold water. Bring to a boil, and immediately lower to a simmer. Cover the pot and let it cook until the meat is just about to fall off the bone but still retains its shape, about 4 hours.

Serve with cider vinegar and hot sauce to pass at the table. Serves 4.

POTATO SALAD DOLL'S WAY

2+1/2 pounds medium boiling potatoes (round white or round red), scrubbed

3 large eggs

1 cup mayonnaise

2 tablespoons brown mustard

1 stalk celery, finely chopped

1/4 cup well-drained sweet relish

1/4 cup roasted pimiento from a jar, diced

1/2 medium onion, finely chopped

1/2 medium green bell pepper, finely chopped

1 clove garlic, minced

1 teaspoon paprika

1 teaspoon dried parsley

1/2 teaspoon celery seeds

1/2 teaspoon salt

1/2 teaspoon freshly ground black pepper

1 dash hot sauce, such as Tabasco, to taste

Place the potatoes in a 6-quart pot and add enough cold water to cover by 2 inches. Bring water to a rapid boil then lower to a medium simmer. Cook until tender when pierced with a fork and skins are just beginning to break, about 35 minutes; add water as necessary to cover potatoes. Drain, and cool completely.

Meanwhile, cook the eggs: Place the eggs in a saucepan and cover with cold water. Bring the water to a rolling boil and remove the pot from the heat. Cover and let stand for 12 minutes. Drain the eggs and cover again with cold water to cool them down.

Peel the cooked, cooled potatoes; cut them into cubes and place in a large bowl. Peel and cube the hard-boiled eggs and add to the bowl.

In a separate bowl, stir together the mayonnaise and mustard. Gently stir the dressing into the potatoes along with the remaining ingredients. Stir to combine with a large wooden spoon, being careful not to mash the potatoes. Chill. Serves 4.

COLLARD GREENS

Doll believed that "you just need greens to be healthy." She lived to age 94. Collards were by far her favorite.

1 ham hock (or 1 smoked turkey wing, or 1 tablespoon corn oil plus 3 dashes Liquid Smoke)

4 pounds (about 4 bunches) collard greens

1/4 cup apple cider vinegar

3 cloves garlic, minced

2 tablespoons onion powder

1 tablespoon sugar

1 tablespoon salt

1 teaspoon freshly ground black pepper

1 teaspoon crushed red pepper flakes

Scrub the ham hock (or turkey wing) and place in a 6-quart pot with enough cold water to cover by several inches. Prepare the greens by removing the tough stems with a knife (discard the stems) then stacking the greens and cutting into 1-inch ribbons. Fill the sink with cold water, add the cut greens, and swish the greens to rinse; change the water at least 3 times. Add the greens to the pot with the ham hock; add all the other ingredients and enough cold water to cover (about 2 quarts). Bring to a boil, then immediately lower to a simmer. Cover and cook for 3 hours, adding enough water to cover as it cooks out. Serves 6 to 8.

GRANDMOTHER MINNIE'S LEMON MERINGUE PIE

SINGLE-CRUST PASTRY

1+1/2 cups sifted all-purpose flour

1/2 teaspoon salt

3 tablespoons cold water

1/2 cup vegetable shortening

FILLING

4 egg yolks, 2 egg whites

1 cup sugar

1 tablespoon all-purpose flour

Juice of 1 large lemon

1 tablespoon grated lemon zest

MERINGUE

4 egg whites

1/4 teaspoon cream of tartar

1/2 cup sugar

Make the crust: Preheat the oven to 475°. Sift 1+1/4 cups of the flour together with the salt into a bowl. Blend the remaining 1/4 cup flour with the water to make a paste. Cut the shortening into the flour and salt, using two knives or a pastry mixer. When the lumps are the size of small peas, add the flour paste. Mix thoroughly but lightly until the mixture can be formed into a ball. Put waxed paper on a counter or board. Place the dough on it and cover with another sheet of waxed paper. Roll with a rolling pin using short, light strokes to make a 12-inch round. Place lightly on a 10-inch pie plate, gently pressing the dough into place. Trim the crust, leaving 1/2 inch beyond the outer edge of the plate. With the tines of a fork, pierce the bottom of the crust twice. Transfer to the oven and bake 8 minutes. Leave the oven on.

Make the filling: Separate the eggs, placing the yolks in a medium double boiler and the whites in a bowl. Beat the yolks until very light. Add 1/2 cup of the sugar and the flour and blend. Add the lemon juice and zest. Cook over medium heat until the mixture thickens, stirring constantly so that it does not scorch. Remove from heat and let cool.

Beat the egg whites until very stiff. Slowly add the remaining 1/2 cup sugar, beating continuously. Add the egg whites to the yolk mixture, folding them in gently. Pour into the pie shell.

Make the meringue: Use an electric hand-mixer to beat all the egg whites with the cream of tartar until they begin to make peaks, adding the sugar a little at a time and beating after each addition. Beat until it forms stiff peaks. Top the filling with the meringue, spreading to form random peaks. Bake the pie for 10 minutes until the meringue is a pretty light golden brown. Serves 6 to 8.

winter

SUNDAY POT ROAST DINNER

“You can bet that just about everyone in Harlem has some kind of roast in the oven for Sunday dinner. Sundays are really special in this community—it's a dress-up, go-to-church, go-home, and be-with-your-folks day. There is always enough to feed a guest or two. A southern pot roast makes the house smell like home—the one you are in, and the one you left behind.”

menu

•

SUNDAY'S BEST SOUTHERN
POT ROAST WITH BROWN GRAVY

•

OVEN-ROASTED POTATOES

•

CARROTS WITH
HONEY AND THYME

•

SAUTÉED KALE

•

AMBROSIA

•

serves 6

SUNDAY'S BEST SOUTHERN POT ROAST WITH BROWN GRAVY

ROAST

1 (5–6-pound) rolled beef rump roast

1/2 cup all-purpose flour

2 teaspoons salt

1 teaspoon freshly ground black pepper

1/4 cup canola oil

3 stalks celery, cut into 4-inch lengths

1 large onion, chopped

3 large cloves garlic, minced

2 bay leaves

1 cup water or beef broth

GRAVY

4 tablespoons fat from pan drippings

3 tablespoons flour mixture (reserved from the roast)

2 cups pan drippings (add water if necessary)

1 tablespoon Worcestershire sauce

1 teaspoon sugar

Salt and freshly ground black pepper, to taste

Make the roast: Preheat the oven to 325°. Rinse the roast, and pat dry with paper towels. Combine the flour, salt, and pepper; reserve 3 tablespoons of this mixture for the gravy, and pat what's left all over the roast. Heat the oil in a large skillet over medium-high heat. Brown the beef on all sides using a long carving fork to turn the meat. Transfer to a roasting pan. Place the celery, onion, garlic, and bay leaves around the beef. Pour the oil from the skillet over the beef. Add water or beef broth, cover, and roast for 3 to 3+1/2 hours, basting every 30 minutes with pan drippings. Let the roast stand for 15 to 20 minutes before carving.

Make the gravy: Remove the roast from the pan and place it on a large platter. Strain the drippings into a measuring cup. Let the drippings stand until the fat rises to the top. Skim the fat, reserving 4 tablespoons and discarding the rest. Heat the reserved fat in the skillet you used to brown the roast. Stir in the reserved flour mixture a little at a time, using a wire whisk or fork, blending until smooth. Cook and stir over low heat until well browned. Add the pan drippings a little at a time, whisking continuously. Continue to cook and stir until thickened and smooth. Stir in Worcestershire, sugar, salt, and pepper. Transfer to a sauceboat and serve with the roast. Serves 6 to 8.

OVEN-ROASTED POTATOES

In the spring you can find small new potatoes in the market. Otherwise, cut larger potatoes into one-inch cubes. These are not roasted in the beef pan, but alone; the texture is more interesting when they're not mixed with the pan drippings.

1 teaspoon garlic powder

1 teaspoon onion powder

1 teaspoon dried parsley

1 teaspoon dried rosemary

1 teaspoon coarse salt

1/2 teaspoon freshly ground black pepper

1/2 cup extra-virgin olive oil, canola oil, or corn oil

3 pounds small new red or white potatoes

Preheat the oven to 425°. In a medium bowl, mix the garlic powder, onion powder, parsley, rosemary, salt, and pepper, and combine with the oil. Pour the mixture into a large plastic bag. Put the scrubbed potatoes in the plastic bag; turn several times to coat the potatoes. Empty the contents, including the marinade, into a pan large enough to hold the potatoes in a single layer. Put the potatoes in the oven the last 45 to 60 minutes of the pot roast's cooking time, and roast, stirring occasionally, until the potatoes are crisp on the outside and tender on the inside. Serves 6 to 8.

CARROTS WITH HONEY AND THYME

8 carrots, peeled, and cut on the diagonal 1/4-inch thick

1 teaspoon honey

1 teaspoon dried thyme

Salt and freshly ground black pepper, to taste

Put the carrots, honey, thyme, salt, and pepper in a saucepan with enough water to cover. Cover and bring to a boil; lower the heat and simmer until tender, 20 to 25 minutes; drain. Serve hot. Serves 6.

SAUTÉED KALE

1 teaspoon canola oil

1 medium onion, cut into small dice

2 cloves garlic, minced

3 or 4 bunches kale, stems removed, leaves rinsed and cut into large strips

1/2 cup water

1/4 teaspoon crushed red pepper flakes

Salt and freshly ground black pepper, to taste

Heat the oil in a large cast-iron skillet over medium heat. Add the onion and garlic and sweat until translucent. Add the kale and sauté until the kale is wilted and dark green, 10 minutes. If the kale is not tender enough, add water a little at a time, and continue sautéing. Season with red pepper, salt, and black pepper. Serves 6.

AMBROSIA

1 fresh pineapple, cored and cut into chunks, or canned in syrup

6 large oranges, peeled and cut into 8 wedges per orange

6 kiwis, pared and sliced

1 cup orange-pineapple juice, or to taste

2 tablespoons Grand Marnier or other orange-flavored liqueur (optional)

1/2 cup sweetened coconut flakes

Layer the pineapple, oranges, and kiwi in a clear glass bowl. In a separate bowl, mix the orange-pineapple juice and Grand Marnier or other orange-flavored liqueur and pour over the fruit. Top with the coconut. Refrigerate until well chilled. Serves 6.

"SUNDAY"

winter

A CHRISTMAS

"My friends Frances and Charles Blackwell and their children, Lisa and David, lived in a beautiful historical landmark house in the Hamilton Heights section of Harlem. Every Christmas, Frances would make this delicious roast."

menu

•

COQUITO

•

BOURBON-MARINATED ROAST BEEF
WITH MUSHROOM SAUCE

•

BRUSSELS SPROUTS

•

ROASTED-GARLIC MASHED POTATOES

•

ENDIVE AND WATERCRESS SALAD
WITH VINAIGRETTE

•

LOSSIE (DOLL) LAWRENCE'S
FRUITCAKE

•

suggested drink:
SEQUOIA GROVE
CABERNET SAUVIGNON

•

serves 8

COQUITO

Harlem is a community steeped in tradition, and if you're Puerto Rican, or if you know your Puerto Rican neighbors, you know that they hold true to theirs. That's why, when Irene Vargas swore she saw a miniature sleigh—and was it eight reindeer flying in the sky over Lenox Avenue?—we all knew she had been up, not hanging stockings, but making coquito. This traditional Puerto Rican version of egg nog is so strong it would make Santa forget to make his drop down your chimney.

1 (15-ounce) can cream of coconut

1 (14-ounce) can sweetened condensed milk

1 (5-ounce) can evaporated milk

1 teaspoon cinnamon

5 egg yolks

3 cups Bacardi 80- or 151-proof dark rum

Grated fresh nutmeg, for garnish

Combine the cream of coconut, sweetened condensed milk, evaporated milk, cinnamon, egg yolks, and rum in a large bowl; pour into a blender in batches, mixing for 10 to 20 seconds. Pour into clean containers, cover, and chill. Serve with a grating of fresh nutmeg. Serves 8.

Note: Pregnant women, the elderly, and people with compromised immune systems should not consume raw eggs.

BOURBON-MARINATED ROAST BEEF

7 pounds boneless beef rib roast

2 cloves garlic, finely minced

1 cup soy sauce

1+1/2 tablespoons red wine vinegar

1/4 cup bourbon

1 cup water

Rinse the rib roast and pat dry with paper towels. Combine the garlic, soy sauce, vinegar, bourbon, and water in a bowl. Place the roast in a large plastic bag, and pour the marinade over the roast. Tie the bag, and turn the roast in the marinade until it's coated on all sides. Place in the refrigerator to marinate overnight, turning once or twice.

Remove the beef from the marinade (discard marinade), pat it dry, and let it come to room temperature. Preheat the oven to 500°. Place the beef on a rack in a roasting pan and roast for 15 minutes. Reduce heat to 350° and roast for 12 minutes more per pound (about 1+1/2 hours) for medium rare; an instant-read thermometer inserted in the thickest part of the roast should read 125°. Transfer the beef to a cutting board and let stand for 30 minutes before slicing. Serves 8.

MUSHROOM SAUCE

Make the sauce while the beef is roasting.

1 tablespoon vegetable oil

1/2 pound white mushrooms, sliced

4 cups canned beef broth

4 teaspoons arrowroot or 2 tablespoons cornstarch

1/4 cup cold water

Salt and freshly ground black pepper, to taste

In a large heavy skillet heat the oil over medium-high heat until it is hot. Sauté the mushrooms, stirring, until they begin to give off their juices, 1 to 2 minutes. Add the broth bring the liquid to a boil, and cook until it is reduced to about 2+1/2 cups, about 20 minutes. Dissolve the arrowroot or cornstarch in the water and stir into the sauce. Simmer until it has thickened, about 3 minutes. Season with salt and pepper and transfer to a sauceboat. Serves 8.

ENDIVE AND WATERCRESS SALAD WITH VINAIGRETTE

5 firm Belgian endives

2 large bunches watercress

2 tablespoons red wine vinegar

1/4 teaspoon salt

1/4 teaspoon freshly ground black pepper

1/2 teaspoon Worcestershire sauce

1/3 cup extra-virgin olive oil

Cut off the root end of the endive, then cut the bulb into 1-inch sections and separate the sections into leaves. Trim the coarse stems from the watercress. Rinse the endive and watercress and spin dry. In a salad bowl, toss the watercress and endive together.

Make the vinaigrette: Whisk together the vinegar, salt, pepper, Worcestershire, and oil. Drizzle the vinaigrette over the salad and toss. Serves 8.

BRUSSELS SPROUTS

4 cups Brussels sprouts, cleaned and trimmed

5 cups water

3 tablespoons unsalted butter, cut into pieces

Salt, to taste

1/2 teaspoon freshly ground black pepper

Score an "X" into the bottom of each sprout with a small sharp knife. In a large saucepan, bring the water to a boil, add salt, and drop in the sprouts. Simmer for 15 minutes, until tender; drain. Put the sprouts back in the still warm pot and add the butter, salt, and pepper. When the butter has melted, toss lightly and serve immediately. Serves 8.

ROASTED-GARLIC MASHED POTATOES

2 medium heads garlic

2 tablespoons olive oil

4 pounds Yukon gold potatoes or russet potatoes

4 tablespoons (1/2 stick) unsalted butter or margarine, softened

2 teaspoons salt

1/2 teaspoon white pepper

1 cup milk or half-and-half or light cream, warmed

2/3 cup sour cream at room temperature

Preheat the oven to 350°. Rub most of the papery skin off of the heads of garlic. With a sharp knife, cut off the top 1/3 of the garlic heads. Rub olive oil all over the garlic heads. Wrap in aluminum foil, sealing the garlic in completely. Place directly on the oven rack and roast until the garlic is soft, about 45 minutes to 1 hour.

After the garlic has been roasting for 15 minutes, peel the potatoes and cut them into large chunks. Place them in a large saucepan and add enough cold water to cover. Bring to a boil, and then reduce heat to a simmer. Partly cover and cook until the potatoes are tender, about 25 minutes. Drain and return to the still hot pot.

When the garlic is done, hold each head upside down and squeeze the garlic cloves out into a saucer; mash with 1 tablespoon of the softened butter.

Add the remaining 3 tablespoons butter or margarine, and the salt and pepper to the potatoes. Using a potato masher, mash the potatoes until there are no lumps. Gently mash in the milk and then the sour cream. Switch to a wooden spoon, and stir in the mashed, roasted garlic. Season with salt and pepper. Serves 8.

LOSSIE (DOLL) LAWRENCE'S FRUITCAKE

Fruitcake is much better if made a few weeks in advance. Indeed, no more than one week after every Thanksgiving, I would observe mother get out her time-worn shopping list and notes. I would watch, help, sneak a taste of my favorite fruits, and question why she had to add the ones I didn't care for. She would just smile and continue on her mission. The thought of those cakes sitting there for weeks was torturous, but everyone knew that they were not to be touched until Christmas Day.

1/2 cup chopped glacéed (candied) cherries

1+1/2 cups chopped glacéed (candied) pineapple

3 cups seedless black raisins

1+1/2 cups dried black currants

1 cup finely chopped dried figs

2 cups broken pecans

1+1/2 cups chopped blanched almonds

1 cup bourbon, cognac, or rum

1 cup (2 sticks) butter, softened, plus more for pans

2+1/2 cups all-purpose flour

1+3/4 cups sugar

6 eggs, separated

2 teaspoons baking powder

3/4 teaspoon baking soda

1 tablespoon grated fresh nutmeg

1 tablespoon cinnamon

1+1/2 teaspoons ground ginger

1+1/2 teaspoons ground mace

1 cup orange juice

1/2 cup quince, apricot, or grape jelly

Combine the cherries, pineapple, raisins, currants, figs, pecans, and almonds in a bowl, and add 1/2 cup of the liquor. Cover with plastic wrap and let stand overnight.

Preheat the oven to 250°. This recipe makes 4 quarts of batter, so you'll need several pans. I use two standard 9x5x2-inch Teflon loaf pans plus an 8+1/2x4+1/2x3-inch loaf pan. Butter the pans well. Line them with a double layer of waxed paper or one layer of parchment paper, and grease the paper with melted butter.

Empty the fruits onto a flat surface and sprinkle with 1/2 cup of the flour. Toss to coat the fruits and nuts, and set aside.

Put the butter in the bowl of an electric mixer. Add the sugar and start beating first on low and then on high speed. Cream the mixture well until it is light in color, about 2 minutes. Beat in the egg yolks one at a time.

Meanwhile, combine the remaining 2 cups flour with the baking powder, baking soda, nutmeg, cinnamon, ginger, and mace; sift together.

Gradually beat the flour mixture into the butter-sugar mixture. Gradually beat in the orange juice and the remaining 1/2 cup liquor. Fold in the floured fruit and the jelly.

Beat the egg whites in a clean, dry bowl with an electric mixer until they form stiff peaks. Fold them into the batter.

Pour the batter into the prepared pans, leaving at least 1 inch of space from the top of the pan. Bake for 2+1/2 hours at 250°, then increase the heat to 275°. The smaller loaf pans should bake for a total of about 3+1/4 hours, the larger ones for 3+1/2 hours. The cake is done when a toothpick inserted into the middle comes out clean. If using an instant-read thermometer, it should register 160°.

When the cakes are removed from the oven, cool on a rack for at least 30 minutes. Run a knife around the edges, and while they're still warm invert them on a rack. They shouldn't stick on the bottom, but if they do, scrape out the stuck portion and repair the bottom with that.

Makes one 2+1/4-pound loaf and two 3-pound loaves.

Note: These cakes can be kept for days, weeks, months. Store in covered cake tins or several layers of aluminum foil in the refrigerator. Douse them occasionally with 1/2 cup bourbon, cognac, or rum.

winter

KWANZAA

"Kwanzaa is a cultural celebration observed by more than 7 million African Americans and other descendants of Africa throughout the world. The holiday, which runs from December 26 through January 1, was created by Dr. Maulana (Ron) Karenga, who chose the Swahili word meaning "first fruits of the harvest" as the name for the celebration. The idea behind the holiday is to strengthen family and community bonds; to draw attention to the past, present, and future of Africans; and to establish a code that benefits the celebrants throughout the year."

menu

•

SENEGALESE CHICKEN YASSA
WITH RICE

•

MUSTARD GREENS

•

FRIED PLANTAINS

•

RITA'S CARROT CAKE

•

COLLIN'S SORREL DRINK

•

serves 6

This holiday is based on Nguzo Saba (The Seven Principles) which are celebrated over the seven-day period: Umoja (Unity); Kujichagulia (Self-Determination); Ujima (Collective Work and Responsibility); Ujamaa (Cooperative Economics); Nia (Purpose); Kuumba (Creativity); Imani (Faith). Like all holidays, there is a time to feast. The Kwanzaa Karamu (feast) is celebrated in the evening of the sixth day. This is a communal feast, and all of the guests bring a dish that represents the cuisine of their culture.

SENEGALESE CHICKEN YASSA WITH RICE

Juice of 4 lemons or limes (1/2 cup)

4 large onions, chopped

2 cloves garlic, minced

1 Scotch bonnet pepper, seeded and chopped fine (see Note)

5 tablespoons canola or olive oil, plus more for broiler rack

1 (3-pound) broiler/fryer chicken, cut into 8 pieces

1/2 cup water

Salt and freshly ground black pepper, to taste

Long-grain white rice

In a bowl large enough to hold all of the chicken, combine the lemon juice, onions, garlic, Scotch bonnet pepper, and 3 tablespoons of the oil. Add the chicken, turning to coat each piece. Cover and refrigerate overnight.

Preheat the broiler and lightly oil the broiler rack. Drain the chicken, reserving the marinade, and arrange it on the rack; broil briefly, until all pieces are just lightly browned on all sides.

In a large skillet, heat the remaining 2 tablespoons oil. Remove the onions from the marinade and discard marinade. Sauté the onions until tender, about 5 minutes. Add the browned chicken and stir in the water. Simmer until the chicken is cooked through, about 30 minutes. Season with salt and pepper.

Meanwhile, cook the rice according to package directions for 6 people. Serve the chicken over hot rice. Serves 4 to 6.

Note: Wash hands immediately after handling these very hot peppers and avoid contact with your eyes and skin.

MUSTARD GREENS

My most beloved ancestor is my mother, Lossie "Doll" Lawrence, and I celebrate her at this feast. I remember that she always laughed and said "the pot likker is for me." Pot likker is the cooking liquid that has absorbed the seasonings and all of the nutrients from the greens and is the cook's prize.

6 bunches (about 6 pounds) mustard greens

1 cup water

1 onion, diced

1 clove garlic, minced

2 tablespoons vegetable oil

3 to 4 dashes Liquid Smoke

Dash of crushed red pepper flakes

Salt and freshly ground black pepper, to taste

Rinse the greens several times; pull the leaves off the heavy stems and discard stems.

In a large pot place the greens, water, onion, garlic, vegetable oil, Liquid Smoke, and crushed red pepper. Cook over low to medium heat for 2 hours stirring every 1/2 hour. The greens should be covered by 1 inch of water. Add water as needed. When the greens are tender, season with salt and pepper. Serves 6.

FRIED PLANTAINS

From Africa to the Caribbean to here in Harlem, the simplest way to prepare plantains is to fry them. They are the perfect accompaniment for almost every meat dish.

4 tablespoons (1/2 stick) unsalted butter

1/4 cup canola oil

6 ripe plantains (black, but firm)

Melt the butter and oil in a skillet and remove from the heat. Peel the plantains and cut on the diagonal into 1+1/2-inch pieces. Reheat the oil and butter and add the plantain pieces, turning and frying over medium heat until they are golden brown. Serve warm. They can be prepared ahead and reheated in the oven in a foil-covered pan. Serves 6.

RITA'S CARROT CAKE

In keeping with the spirit of Kwanzaa, all food should be prepared at home. This ensures that all seven principles play a part in the feast. Some things are worth the effort, and a home-baked cake is one of them. From my father's side of the family, my niece Rita is the only one who can rival the good cooks in my mother's family.

CAKE

Butter, softened, for pans

3 cups sifted all-purpose flour, plus more for pans

2 teaspoons baking powder

1 teaspoon baking soda

2 teaspoons cinnamon

1 teaspoon salt

2 cups sugar

1+1/2 cups canola oil

4 eggs

1 pound carrots, peeled and grated (3 cups)

WHIPPED CREAM FROSTING

2 cups heavy cream, chilled

1/2 cup unsifted confectioners' sugar

1 teaspoon pure vanilla extract

Pecan halves, for decorating

Make the cake: Preheat the oven to 350°. Butter and flour three deep, round 9-inch cake pans.

Sift the flour, baking powder, baking soda, cinnamon, and salt together. In a large mixing bowl, with an electric mixer at medium speed, beat the sugar, oil, and eggs until well blended, 2 minutes. Add the carrots and mix well. Gradually add the flour mixture, beating at low speed until well combined. The batter will look a bit thin. Pour the batter into the prepared pans, dividing equally. Bake until a toothpick inserted into the middle comes out clean, 30 to 35 minutes.

Cool in pans on a rack, 20 minutes. Carefully loosen the sides with a spatula, remove from pans, and cool completely.

Make the frosting: In a clean dry bowl, whip the cream with the confectioners' sugar and vanilla until stiff. Refrigerate if not using immediately.

Put one layer of cake on a cake platter and spread the top with 3/4 cup frosting. Top with another layer and spread another 3/4 cup frosting on the top. Repeat with the third layer, then frost the sides and top. Arrange the pecan halves on top. Refrigerate several hours before serving. Makes one 9-inch, 3-layer cake.

COLLIN'S SORREL DRINK

We would never celebrate this holiday without inviting Collin Julian Clarke, my neighbor a few doors down, who is also my friend, surrogate son, party planner, and would-be manager of my life (if he cares about you, he will readily manage yours). Collin calls religiously to ask, "What are you cooking today?" Once told, he will either say, "I'm not feeling it" or, if he is feeling it, he'll just ring the bell around dinner time. Collin is true to the Caribbean food he knew growing up in Guyana. We leave it to him to bring his sorrel drink for the Kwanzaa feast. In Africa and in the Caribbean this fragrant drink is served regularly, but particularly on holidays. This sorrel is not the kind found commonly in the United States, but is rather the red dried blossoms of the sorrel tree, more often called the hibiscus tree (hibiscus sabdariffa). It can be found wherever African and West Indian foods are sold. Or it may be ordered from the Angel Brand Co., Box 191, Media, PA 19063; telephone: 610-565-3460.

5 ounces dried sorrel (dried hibiscus flowers), picked over and rinsed

12 cloves

4 cinnamon sticks

2 tablespoons grated fresh ginger

2 quarts water

Ice cubes

Sugar, to taste

Fresh mint sprigs, for garnish (optional)

Lemon slices, for garnish (optional)

Rum (optional)

Place the sorrel, cloves, cinnamon sticks, ginger, and water in a large pot and bring to a boil. Reduce the heat to low and simmer for 30 minutes. Steep, at room temperature, for 24 hours in a large covered jar or bowl. Strain, and pour into a large covered bottle; refrigerate.

To serve, fill a pitcher half full with steeped sorrel, add 1/3 more cold water, then ice cubes. Add sugar to taste, and stir. Garnish glasses with a slice of lemon or fresh mint sprig. Don't be afraid to add rum to the glass. Serves 6.

winter

NEW YEAR'S DAY

"If you really want to celebrate New Year's, you must come to Harlem. We do it in church—and if you don't think so, just go to Abyssinian Baptist Church, or St. John the Divine, or any of the many churches in the area. We are a spiritual community. We also do it at home, on a grand scale or with small groups of family and friends. We are a partying community. Pork is the meat of choice in Harlem for New Year's Day. Any cut, cooked any way, depending on your roots."

menu

•

CUBAN ROAST PORK
WITH LIME

•

HOPPIN' JOHN
(BLACK-EYED PEAS)
WITH RICE

•

MIXED GREENS

•

SWEET POTATO PIE

•

suggested drink:

POMMERY BRUT ROSÉ
CHAMPAGNE NV

•

serves 6

CUBAN ROAST PORK WITH LIME

1/2 cup fresh lime juice

3 large cloves garlic, chopped

1 tablespoon dried oregano, crumbled

1/2 teaspoon freshly ground black pepper

1 (4-to-5-pound) boneless pork loin

1+1/2 teaspoons salt

In a bowl just large enough to hold the pork, combine the lime juice, garlic, oregano, and pepper. Coat the pork in the marinade, cover it, and put it in the refrigerator to marinate overnight, turning once or twice.

Let the pork come to room temperature, and preheat the oven to 350°. Transfer the pork to a roasting pan, discarding the marinade. Season with salt. Roast the pork, covered loosely with aluminum foil, in the middle of the oven, 1 hour. Remove the foil and continue roasting for 90 minutes more; an instant-read thermometer inserted into the thickest part of the roast should read 150° to 155°. Transfer the pork to a platter and let stand 20 minutes before carving. Serves 6.

HOPPIN' JOHN (BLACK-EYED PEAS) WITH RICE

We were blessed to be able to visit the motherland 35 years ago and to bond with good people who became family. On our trip to Ghana, West Africa, we met Mizpah and Barton Glymin Sr. and their children, and our friendship has been one of life's rewards. Over the years they have made several trips to Harlem, and I have gone to Ghana to visit them, too. Whenever I get my pot going, my thoughts go straight to Africa. My last visit was to celebrate the life of Barton Sr. with his grieving widow. Black-eyed peas were served that day. Acaraje is a black-eyed pea fritter prepared in Brazil; akara is a similar fritter, cooked in Nigeria. Black-eyed peas are prepared throughout the Caribbean; here in the U.S. the dish is referred to as Hoppin' John, and to date no one has been able to agree upon the origin of this name. What we do believe is that to have black-eyed peas on New Year's Day will bring good luck in the coming year.

1 pound dried black-eyed peas

1 large ham hock

1 large onion, finely chopped

3 cloves garlic, minced

2 bay leaves

1/2 teaspoon dried thyme, crushed

1/2 teaspoon crushed red pepper flakes

1 tablespoon salt

3 grinds fresh black pepper

1/4 cup dry sherry

Long-grain white rice

Place the black-eyed peas in a large pot with enough water to cover by 3 inches, and let them soak overnight.

Place the ham hock in a saucepan with enough water to cover. Bring to a boil, and reduce to a simmer. Add the onions, garlic, bay leaves, thyme, crushed red pepper, salt, pepper, and sherry. Simmer until the ham hocks are tender, 2+1/2 to 3 hours. Remove the ham hock and set aside. Drain and rinse the peas and add to the ham liquid. Bring to a boil and simmer, covered, until the beans are tender, 45 minutes to 1 hour.

Remove the plug of ham from the hock, and crumble it into the beans. Discard the bone and fat of the hock. If the beans need more liquid, add just enough water to cover. If they're too watery, turn the heat up and simmer, uncovered, until they're the consistency you want.

Make enough rice for 6 to 8 people, according to the package directions. Serve Hoppin' John over hot rice. Serves 6 to 8.

MIXED GREENS

Everyone has their favorite greens, so if you mix them, you are sure to please everyone. The combination also makes the greens more interesting in terms of texture and flavor.

2 pounds collard greens

2 pounds kale

2 pounds mustard greens

1/4 teaspoon crushed red pepper flakes

1/4 teaspoon freshly ground black pepper

1 tablespoon salt

3 dashes Liquid Smoke

1 tablespoon white vinegar

1 tablespoon sugar

1/4 cup olive oil

5 to 6 cups water

Greens are usually quite gritty, so rinse them well, changing the water several times. Remove them to a colander. Remove all the stems, stack the greens, and cut on the diagonal into wide strips. Place the greens in a large pot, and add the red pepper flakes, black pepper, salt, Liquid Smoke, vinegar, sugar, olive oil, and water. Cover and bring to a boil; as the greens wilt, stir and let them wilt a bit more. If necessary add greens in batches until they all fit in. Bring the temperature down, and let simmer until the greens are tender, about 1+1/2 hours, stirring occasionally. Correct salt and pepper and other seasonings to taste. Serves 6.

SWEET POTATO PIE

Girls, listen up! If you don't know how to make sweet potato pie, you aren't in the running. As you get more experience, you will be adding your own thing. It may be shredded coconut, or bourbon, or a pecan topping. But first you must learn to make a basic sweet potato pie, because you can bet that his mother knew how, and he will be waiting to see what you can do.

PIECRUST

1 cup all-purpose flour, plus more for dusting

1/4 teaspoon salt

3 tablespoons unsalted butter, chilled and cut into small pieces

2 tablespoons vegetable shortening chilled

1/4 cup ice water

FILLING

1+1/2 pounds deep red-gold sweet potatoes or Louisiana yams

1/2 cup sugar

2 large eggs, beaten

2 tablespoons unsalted butter, melted

1 teaspoon grated fresh nutmeg

1/2 teaspoon cinnamon

1/2 teaspoon ground ginger

1/8 teaspoon ground cloves

1/4 teaspoon salt

1 teaspoon pure vanilla extract

1/4 cup milk

Whipped cream or vanilla ice cream, for serving

Make the crust: In a large bowl, combine the flour and salt. Using 2 knives or a pastry blender, cut the butter and shortening into the flour until the mixture resembles coarse meal. Sprinkle in the water. Mix with a fork, tossing until the dough is moist enough to form a ball. You may have to add a bit more water. Flatten the dough into a disk, wrap with plastic wrap, and refrigerate for a minimum of 1 hour, and for up to 2 days.

Prepare the filling. In a saucepan of boiling water, simmer the sweet potatoes until soft when pierced with a knife, about 30 minutes. Drain, then rinse under cold water. Let them cool; remove the skins, then mash. You should have 2 cups of mashed sweet potatoes.

In a large bowl, whisk together the sugar, eggs, and melted butter until smooth. Add the mashed sweet potatoes, and blend; add the nutmeg, cinnamon, ginger, cloves, salt, and vanilla. Stir in the milk gradually.

Preheat the oven to 350°. Remove the chilled dough and let it stand for 10 minutes. Roll the dough on a floured board into an 11-inch round; ease it into a 9-inch pie pan, pressing it into the bottom and up the sides. Trim the dough with scissors, and flute the edges with a fork or your fingers. Fill the pie shell with the sweet potato mixture. Bake in the lower third of the oven just until set, or until a toothpick or knife inserted halfway down into the center comes out clean, 55 to 60 minutes. Let the pie cool, and it will firm up. Serve warm or at room temperature, with whipped cream or vanilla ice cream. Serves 6 to 8.

winter

DR. MARTIN LUTHER KING JR.'S BIRTHDAY

"Harlem celebrates this day (January 19th) in many of its churches or at home with a meaningful meal—and for many of us this means soul food: We remember what nourished us when there was nothing else, and how the inventiveness and skill of the ancestors contributed to our culture with this special cuisine."

menu

•

BARBECUED PORK NECK BONES
WITH BOURBON-MUSTARD SAUCE

•

TURNIP GREENS

•

TWICE-BAKED POTATOES

•

CLASSIC PEACH COBBLER

•

serves 6

BARBECUED PORK NECK BONES

It is said that the sweetest meat is nearer the bone. Well now, this saying isn't necessarily only about a skinny person—if you dine on a sparerib, a pork chop bone, or a neck bone, you know what they're talking about. But you need a whole plateful of neck bones to get to the sweet meat, because there is so little of it. It's worth every nibble. When buying neck bones allow at least 1+1/2 pounds per person. If it sounds like a lot, trust me, it isn't.

6 pounds fresh pork neck bones

1 tablespoon chili powder

1 tablespoon dry mustard

1 tablespoon kosher salt

1 teaspoon cayenne pepper

1 teaspoon cinnamon

Bourbon-Mustard Sauce (recipe follows)

Rinse the neck bones and pat dry with a paper towel. Combine the chili powder, mustard, salt, cayenne pepper, and cinnamon and rub the mixture all over the bones. Cover with plastic wrap and refrigerate overnight.

Allow bones to reach room temperature. Preheat the oven to 350°. Place the bones on the rack of a baking pan, cover with aluminum foil, and bake for 1 hour. This dish can be prepared up to this point, the day before serving or earlier the same day. Remove the rack from the pan, leaving the neck bones on the bottom of the pan. Pour the Bourbon-Mustard Sauce over the neck bones, cover loosely with foil, and bake for an additional 30 minutes. Serves 4 to 6.

BOURBON-MUSTARD SAUCE

This barbecue sauce can be prepared up two weeks ahead and stored, covered, in the refrigerator.

1 tablespoon vegetable oil

1 bunch scallions, the white parts, chopped

4 cloves garlic, finely minced

1 cup packed golden brown sugar

1/2 cup ketchup

1/2 cup tomato paste

1/2 cup Dijon mustard

1/2 cup water

1/4 cup Worcestershire sauce

1/4 cup cider vinegar

1/2 teaspoon cumin

1/2 cup bourbon

Salt and freshly ground black pepper, to taste

Heat the oil in a large heavy saucepan over medium-low heat. Add the scallions and garlic and sauté until tender, 10 to 15 minutes; do not burn–if it's cooking too fast, turn the heat down. In a saucepan, combine the brown sugar, ketchup, tomato paste, mustard, water, Worcestershire, vinegar, and cumin; stir in the bourbon. Simmer the sauce until thick and reduce to 3+1/2 cups, stirring occasionally, about 1 hour. Season with salt and pepper. Makes 3+1/2 cups.

TURNIP GREENS

2 slices bacon

6 bunches turnip greens, leaves stripped from stems, rinsed several times, chopped coarsely

2 tablespoons sugar

1 tablespoon cider vinegar

1 teaspoon crushed red pepper flakes

2/3 cup water

In a large heavy saucepan, cook the bacon over low heat until translucent. Add the greens to the pot along with the sugar, vinegar, red pepper flakes, and water. Stir, cover, and simmer over low heat for 3 hours. The bacon will not be crisp after cooking with the greens, but it should be put into the serving bowl, as some do like it this way. Serves 6.

TWICE-BAKED POTATOES

6 large Idaho potatoes, scrubbed

1/2 cup (1 stick) unsalted butter

1/2 pint sour cream

1 tablespoon dried chives

Salt and white pepper to taste

Preheat the oven to 400°. Wrap each potato in aluminum foil. Place the potatoes on the lower rack of the oven, and bake for 1 hour. Remove the potatoes from the oven and lower the heat to 350°. Let the potatoes sit until just cool enough to handle but not cold.

Unwrap the foil, cut off the top 1/3 of the potato lengthwise. Scoop out the flesh from the cut tops and place in a bowl; discard the skins from the tops. Scoop out the flesh from the potatoes with a spoon (you may wish to run a small knife around the perimeter of the skins to loosen the flesh) and add to the bowl. Mash with a potato masher, and add the butter, sour cream, chives, salt, and white pepper. Fill each potato skin with the mashed potatoes, and rewrap each with fresh foil. The potatoes can be prepared to this point up to a day ahead of time.

Twenty minutes prior to serving the meal, return the potatoes to the 350° oven. Unwrap and serve hot. Serves 6.

CLASSIC PEACH COBBLER

From Adam Clayton Powell Jr. Boulevard up Frederick Douglass Boulevard along St. Nicholas Avenue, and up on Sugar Hill, just about every oven at one time or another has baked a peach cobbler. A cobbler can be baked with a variety of fruits and berries, but peach is the classic.

6 cups sliced fresh or frozen peaches

3/4 cup (1+1/2 sticks) unsalted butter

1 cup sugar

1 cup plus 2 tablespoons self-rising flour

1/2 teaspoon cinnamon

1/2 cup milk

Ice cream, for serving (optional)

Preheat the oven to 350°. Peel, pit, and slice the peaches (thaw if using frozen peaches).

Melt 4 tablespoons of the butter in a medium saucepan over low heat. Add the sliced peaches and 1/2 cup of the sugar. Stir in 2 tablespoons of the flour, and simmer 10 minutes.

In a medium bowl combine the remaining 1/2 cup sugar and the cinnamon with the remaining 1 cup flour. Stir in the milk.

Melt the remaining 8 tablespoons butter and pour it into a 9x13-inch baking pan. Reserve 1/3 cup batter, and pour the rest into the pan. Pour the peach mixture over the top of the batter. Drizzle the remaining batter over the peaches, and spread to cover.

Bake until the top is golden brown, about 1 hour. Serve warm, perhaps with a dollop of vanilla ice cream on top.

winter

HOLIDAY BRUNCH

“Brunch is an elegant way to start the day. Host and guests alike can sleep in, and still indulge in a leisurely meal. Serve this menu with grits prepared according to package directions for 6 people, allowing ample servings for 4.”

menu

•

CHICKEN LIVERS IN
MUSHROOM-WINE SAUCE

•

GRITS

•

SCRAMBLED EGGS

•

FRIED GREEN TOMATOES

•

BISCUITS

•

serves 4

CHICKEN LIVERS IN MUSHROOM-WINE SAUCE

The late Sonny Bostic, a well-known Harlem caterer, did chicken livers like nobody else.

2 tablespoons unsalted butter

1 large onion, coarsely chopped

3 cloves garlic, minced

4 extra-large white mushrooms, cleaned and sliced

1 cup dry red wine or dry sherry

2 pounds chicken livers, picked and cleaned

1/2 cup all-purpose flour

1/4 cup vegetable oil

1 teaspoon salt

1 teaspoon freshly ground black pepper

1 teaspoon cayenne pepper

1/2 pound sliced bacon

Make the mushroom-wine sauce: Melt the butter in a large skillet over low heat. Add the onions and garlic and sauté until the onions are translucent, about 8 minutes. Add the mushrooms and wine and simmer until the mushrooms are soft and have given off their liquid, about 8 minutes. Remove the pan from the heat.

Dredge the chicken livers in the flour, shaking off excess. In another large skillet heat the oil over medium heat. Add the chicken livers, not crowding them, and brown briefly on both sides; do not overcook. Remove the livers with a slotted spatula and add to the mushroom-wine sauce. Turn the heat on low and simmer, covered, 20 minutes.

Meanwhile, fry the bacon in a skillet over medium-high heat; drain on paper towels. Serve the livers garnished with strips of fried bacon. Serves 4.

SCRAMBLED EGGS

The secret to scrambled eggs is to get enough air into them while beating. A wire whisk works well; if you're scrambling a lot of eggs, mix them in a blender. Enough butter in the skillet will not only keep the eggs from sticking to the pan, but will make for creamier eggs.

8 large eggs

2 tablespoons water

3 tablespoons unsalted butter

Beat the eggs with the water using a whisk or a blender. In a 10-inch skillet over low heat, melt the butter, turning the pan so that the sides are coated 1/3 of the way up. Turn the heat up to medium, and immediately pour the eggs into the pan, stirring from the sides and bottom, until cooked. Serves 4.

FRIED GREEN TOMATOES

1 large egg, beaten

1 tablespoon water

3/4 cup Italian bread crumbs

3 large green tomatoes, sliced 1/4-inch thick

1/4 cup vegetable oil

Beat the egg and water in a wide shallow bowl. Place a sheet of waxed paper or aluminum foil on a flat surface and spread the bread crumbs on it. Dip slices of tomato into the egg wash and then coat each side with bread crumbs.

Heat the oil in a large skillet over medium heat. Fry the tomatoes until golden brown and tender, about 3 minutes on each side, turning once. Drain on paper towels and serve hot. Serves 4.

BISCUITS

What is more southern than fluffy biscuits, just dripping with butter?

1 cup all-purpose flour, plus more for dusting

1 heaping teaspoon baking powder

1/2 teaspoon salt

2 heaping tablespoons vegetable shortening

1/2 cup milk

Preheat the oven to 450°. Sift the flour, baking powder, and salt into a bowl. Cut in the shortening with a fork until it resembles fine meal. Add the milk slowly, blending with a wooden spoon just until a dough forms. Do not overbeat.

Dust a sheet of waxed paper with a little flour. Roll out the dough with a rolling pin or the palms of your hands until it is about 1/2-inch thick. Cut out the biscuits with a 3-inch drinking glass or biscuit cutter. Prick the top of each biscuit once with a fork. Place the biscuits on an ungreased sheet pan and bake until they are just beginning to turn golden, 12 to 15 minutes. Makes about 8 biscuits.

SPRING

A DOUGLA FEAST

MENU

•

CHICKEN SALAD DOUGLA

ASPARAGUS WITH VINAIGRETTE

DOLL'S PICKLED BEETS

SOUTHERN SPICED
GINGERBREAD
WITH LEMON SAUCE

suggested drink:
CHABLIS

see recipes page 70

spring

EASTER IN HARLEM

"You haven't been anywhere or seen anything until you experience Easter in Harlem. Our churches are standing room only. The Easter parade up Fifth Avenue pales by comparison to the one put on here, and then there is Easter dinner. After the church service, my neighbor Jewel Johnson does her thing."

menu

•

JEWEL'S SPRING
LEG OF LAMB

•

CURRIED RICE WITH RAISINS

•

ASPARAGUS WITH DRAWN BUTTER

•

MESCLUN SALAD WITH SWEET
MANGO DRESSING

•

VIVIAN'S LEMON-GLAZED CAKE

•

suggested drink:
GEORGES DUBOEUF
BEAUJOLAIS-VILLAGES

•

serves 4 to 6

JEWEL'S SPRING LEG OF LAMB

1 (5- to 6-pound) boneless leg of lamb

2 cloves garlic, thinly sliced

1 teaspoon ground ginger

1 teaspoon dry mustard

2 teaspoons sugar

1 cup strong, hot brewed coffee

2 tablespoons light cream

2 tablespoons green ginger wine or port wine

2 tablespoons all-purpose flour

1/3 cup currant jelly

Salt and freshly ground black pepper, to taste

Make the lamb: Preheat the oven to 350°. Cut 6 to 8 slits in the leg of lamb: insert a sliver of garlic into each slit, as deep as you can get them. Mix the ginger and mustard together, and rub all over the lamb. Place the lamb, fat side up, on a rack in a shallow roasting pan. Roast for 1 hour.

Dissolve the sugar in the hot coffee, stir in the light cream and ginger wine or port wine, and pour the mixture over the lamb. Continue to roast for another 2 to 2+1/2 hours, basting occasionally. Lift the meat onto a warm platter.

Make the sauce: Pour the pan juices into a 2-cup measuring cup and skim off the fat; reserve fat. Add enough water to the pan juices to make 1+1/2 cups. Place the roasting pan over medium-high on the stove. Measure 2 tablespoons of fat back into the pan, blend in the flour, and stir in the meat juices and current jelly. Cook and stir until thick. Season with salt and pepper and pour into a sauceboat. Pass the sauce with the lamb. Serves 4 to 6.

CURRIED RICE WITH RAISINS

2+1/2 cups chicken broth

1/2 teaspoon salt

2 teaspoons curry powder

1 cup long-grain white rice

1/2 cup raisins

Combine the broth, salt, and curry power in a saucepan and bring to a boil. Add the rice, cover, and simmer on low until the rice is tender, 20 to 25 minutes. Stir in the raisins the last 5 minutes of cooking. Serves 4 to 6.

ASPARAGUS WITH DRAWN BUTTER

3 dozen medium asparagus spears

1 cup (2 sticks) unsalted butter

Trim off about 2 inches from the bottoms of the asparagus spears, so that all are of uniform length. Using kitchen string, tie the asparagus into 3 bundles. First tie the bottom third, then just under the tips. Bring a large pot of water to a boil. Add the asparagus and cook until tender, about 5 minutes.

Meanwhile, melt the butter in a heavy saucepan over low heat. Do not boil. Skim off the froth from the top and carefully pour the clear liquid into a bowl or a pan. Discard the milky residue. (This can be done ahead and warmed when the asparagus are done.)

Lift the asparagus out of the saucepan with tongs and place on a sided serving tray. Remove the kitchen string and discard. Pour the drawn butter over the asparagus and serve immediately. Serves 4 to 6.

MESCLUN SALAD WITH SWEET MANGO DRESSING

Good neighbor Carol Turner brings the salad—and this wonderful dressing.

1 very ripe mango

Juice of 1 lime

1 small clove garlic, minced

1 tablespoon Grand Marnier or other orange-flavored liqueur

2 pieces crystallized ginger

3 tablespoons extra-virgin olive oil

1+1/2 pounds salad greens, washed and spun dry

Cut the mango along the flat side of the pit and remove the two halves. Scoop out the pulp and place it in a blender. Add the lime juice, garlic, Grand Marnier or other orange-flavored liqueur, and crystallized ginger and process until smooth. With the blender running, gradually add the oil, blending until completely combined.

Place the mesclun in a salad bowl, pour the dressing over the salad greens and gently toss. Serves 6.

VIVIAN'S LEMON-GLAZED CAKE

CAKE

4 eggs

1 box (18.25 ounces) yellow cake mix

1 (3+5/8-ounce) package instant lemon pudding mix

3/4 cup water

1/2 cup corn oil

GLAZE

1/3 cup fresh lemon juice

2 cups sifted confectioners' sugar

Preheat the oven following package instructions. Make the cake: Beat the eggs until thick and lemon-colored, 3 to 4 minutes. Add the cake mix, pudding mix, water, and oil. Beat with an electric mixer at medium speed for 10 minutes. Pour into a 10-inch spring-form pan. Bake until a toothpick inserted in the middle comes out clean, about 50 minutes, and place on a rack. When cool enough to handle, remove the spring-form, and place the cake on a cake platter. Using a long two-tined fork, prick holes in the top of the cake.

Make the glaze: Combine the lemon juice and sugar in a saucepan. Heat just to a boil. Drizzle the glaze over the top of the cake while it is still hot and spread around the sides. Makes one single-layer 10-inch cake.

"APOLLO"

spring

A DOUGLA FEAST

"In Trinidad, the offspring of Africans and Hindus are called "Dougla." The electrifying ballet Dougla—performed by the Dance Theatre of Harlem, and for which Geoffrey Holder choreographed, costume-designed, and created the music—inspired this meal."

menu

•

CHICKEN SALAD DOUGLA

•

ASPARAGUS WITH VINAIGRETTE

•

DOLL'S PICKLED BEETS

•

SOUTHERN SPICED GINGERBREAD
WITH LEMON SAUCE

•

suggested drink:
CHABLIS

•

serves 8

CHICKEN SALAD DOUGLA

Mango chutney is available in specialty food stores and large supermarkets.

8 large chicken breast halves

2 stalks celery, peeled and halved

2 large carrots, peeled and halved

1 onion, peeled and quartered

2 bay leaves

1 tablespoon salt

1 teaspoon freshly ground black pepper

3 cloves garlic

1/2 bunch broccoli, cut into florets (1+1/4 cups)

1 Red Delicious apple

1+1/2 cups mayonnaise

1 (12-ounce) jar mango chutney

3 teaspoons curry powder

In a 6-quart pot, place the chicken breasts, celery, carrots, onion, bay leaves, salt, pepper, and garlic, and cover with water; bring to a boil then lower to a simmer. Cook until the chicken is done, 45 minutes to 1 hour, adding water as it cooks out. Remove the chicken with a slotted spoon, cool, and refrigerate until chilled thoroughly, several hours. Remove all skin and bones and cut the meat into 1-inch cubes.

Bring a saucepan full of water to a boil. Add the broccoli and blanch for 1 to 2 minutes, then plunge into cold water. Drain and chill.

Core and dice the apple. In a bowl, mix together the mayonnaise, chutney, and curry powder. Add to the diced chicken. Add the broccoli and apple. Gently mix all together and chill until ready to serve. Serves 8.

ASPARAGUS WITH VINAIGRETTE

Choose asparagus that are young and tender. The tips should be tight and the spears firm.

4 dozen medium asparagus spears

2 tablespoons Dijon mustard

1/4 cup red wine vinegar

1 cup extra-virgin olive oil

1/4 teaspoon salt

1/4 teaspoon freshly ground black pepper

Trim the asparagus. Using kitchen string, tie them into 4 bundles of 12. First the bottom third, then just under the tips.

Fill a 6-quart pot with water and bring to a boil; add salt. Lower the asparagus into the water, cover, and cook for 8 minutes. Meanwhile, prepare an ice-water bath. Lift the asparagus out with a tongs, and immerse in ice water for a few minutes. Drain, and chill in the refrigerator on a glass or plastic tray.

Make the vinaigrette: Combine the mustard, vinegar, olive oil, salt, and pepper in a medium bowl. Whisk until well combined. Pour over the asparagus and chill until ready to serve. Serves 8.

DOLL'S PICKLED BEETS

4 (15-ounce) cans sliced beets

2 medium onions, thinly sliced and separated into rings

1+1/2 cups sugar

2 cups white vinegar

1 cup water

1/4 cup lemon juice

1 teaspoon salt

Drain and rinse the beets and place them in a glass bowl. Add the onions to the beets. Combine the sugar, vinegar, water, lemon juice, and salt in a saucepan and bring to a boil. Lower the heat and simmer, 10 minutes. Pour the pickling liquid over the beets, cover, and chill overnight. Serves 8.

SOUTHERN SPICED GINGERBREAD WITH LEMON SAUCE

GINGERBREAD

1/2 cup vegetable shortening, plus more for pan

1 cup dark molasses

1/2 cup sugar

2 eggs

1/2 cup boiling water

2+1/2 cups all-purpose flour

2 teaspoons baking soda

1/4 teaspoon salt

2 teaspoons ground ginger

1 teaspoon cinnamon

1/2 teaspoon nutmeg

LEMON SAUCE

Grated zest of 2 lemons

3/4 cup fresh lemon juice

1 cup sugar

2 tablespoons cornstarch

4 egg yolks

Make the gingerbread: Preheat the oven to 325°. Grease an 11x9-inch baking pan with vegetable shortening. Beat 1/2 cup shortening, the molasses, sugar, and eggs together in a heatproof bowl. Add the boiling water. In another bowl, sift the dry ingredients together and add to the molasses mixture. Bake until a toothpick inserted into the middle comes out clean, 25 to 30 minutes.

Meanwhile, make the lemon sauce: Boil the lemon zest, lemon juice, 1+1/4 cups water, and sugar together in a saucepan, 5 minutes. Whisk cornstarch with 1/4 cup cold water, and whisk with the egg yolks to form a paste. Add a small amount of the hot lemon-sugar mixture to the egg yolks and blend. Add the yolks to the saucepan and boil again until thick and clear, about 5 minutes.

Cut the gingerbread into 8 pieces. Serve with lemon sauce on the side. Serves 8.

"NEW ARRIVAL"

spring

HOMECOMING

"When my niece Dzifa would come home from college and to my house for dinner, I would cook chicken and rice for her and call the dish Chicken Dzifa. But when she returned and would ask for the same dish, I could never remember how I made it. This, then, is the special recipe, created just for her."

menu

•

CHICKEN DZIFA

•

JAMAICAN PEAS AND RICE

•

TOSSED ICEBERG LETTUCE SALAD
WITH VINAIGRETTE

•

MANGO UPSIDE-DOWN CAKE

•

suggested drink:
GINGER BEER

•

serves 4

CHICKEN DZIFA

1 (3-pound) broiler/fryer chicken, cut into 8 pieces

2 limes

1/4 cup all-purpose flour

1 teaspoon salt

1/2 teaspoon freshly ground black pepper

1/4 cup corn oil or canola oil

2 tablespoons honey

1/2 cup dry sherry

1/4 cup chicken broth

Place the chicken pieces in a shallow baking dish. Grate the zest of one lime and set zest aside. Squeeze the juice of the grated lime over the chicken. Toss to coat, and let stand for 30 minutes.

Preheat the oven to 375°. Place the flour in a shallow dish or a bag and season with salt and pepper. Remove the chicken pieces from the marinade and dredge them in the flour. Heat the oil in a large skillet over medium-high heat and brown the chicken on all sides. Return the chicken to the baking dish. Combine the grated lime zest and honey and drizzle over the chicken. Pour the sherry and broth over the chicken, cover with aluminum foil, and bake for 30 minutes. Slice the remaining lime into thin slices and use as a garnish. Serves 4.

JAMAICAN PEAS AND RICE

Peas and rice are served with almost every Jamaican meal. The peas are actually pigeon beans that originated in Africa. When set before Dzifa, this dish brings a smile to her face.

1 tablespoon olive oil

1 medium onion, diced

2 cloves garlic, finely chopped

2 cups chicken broth

1/2 cup dried pigeon peas, rinsed and soaked, according to package directions

1 cup long-grain rice

1/2 teaspoon ground thyme

1/2 teaspoon ground ginger

1/2 teaspoon allspice

1 teaspoon salt

Heat the oil in a 4-quart saucepan over medium heat, and sauté the onions and garlic until soft. Add the chicken broth and pigeon peas and bring to a boil. Reduce the heat to a simmer, cover, and cook for 40 minutes.

Add the rice, thyme, ginger, allspice, and salt. Stir, cover, and cook until the rice is tender, 20 minutes. If the rice is too dry, add a little water and mix. Serves 4.

TOSSED ICEBERG LETTUCE SALAD WITH VINAIGRETTE

There are a variety of salad greens in the local markets here, but many residents still prefer iceberg lettuce. It is crisp and cold. This is the lettuce used in the South, and the one that we are most familiar with.

1 head iceberg lettuce, leaves separated and torn into bite-size pieces

1/2 green bell pepper, thinly sliced

1 small onion, cut into thin rings

4 plum tomatoes, cut into quarters

1 cup extra-virgin olive oil

1/3 cup tarragon vinegar

1/2 teaspoon salt

1/4 teaspoon freshly ground black pepper

1 teaspoon garlic powder

1/4 teaspoon dry mustard

1/2 teaspoon dried parsley

1/2 teaspoon dried oregano

Place the lettuce, bell pepper, onion, and tomatoes in a large salad bowl and toss gently.

Make the vinaigrette: Combine the oil, vinegar, salt, pepper, garlic powder, mustard, parsley, and oregano in a jar with a lid; cover tightly and shake until blended.

Measure out 1/3 cup vinaigrette and drizzle it over the salad; reserve the rest in the refrigerator for future use. Toss the salad gently and serve. Serves 4 to 6.

MANGO UPSIDE-DOWN CAKE

Does anyone remember M.C. Hammer entertaining us with "Can't Touch This?" Every Southern cook takes pride in their upside-down cake, but as Hammer said. . . .

3 ripe mangoes, peeled

1/2 cup (1 stick) plus 1/3 cup (5+1/3 tablespoons) unsalted butter, softened

3/4 cup firmly packed light brown sugar

1/2 cup dark rum

1+2/3 cups all-purpose flour

2 teaspoons baking powder

2/3 cup granulated sugar

3 eggs

2/3 cup milk

Slice the mangoes in half to the pit and cut the flesh into strips 4 inches long and 1 inch wide; set aside. Melt 1 stick of butter in a skillet over low heat. Add the mangoes and sprinkle with brown sugar. Cook, stirring occasionally with a wooden spoon, until the sugar melts and the fruit is tender but firm, about 5 minutes. Using a slotted spoon, remove the fruit from the skillet, and drain in strainer. Continue cooking the sugar mixture until it reduces to a thick syrup, about 5 minutes more. Remove from heat and add the rum. Carefully ignite with a long wooden match or grill lighter, and let flames die out.

Arrange a single layer of mangoes in a sunburst pattern in an 8-inch cake pan. Add enough syrup to cover the mangoes. Set aside to cool.

Preheat the oven to 350°. In a medium bowl, sift together the flour and baking powder and set aside. In a large bowl, cream the remaining 1/3 cup butter. Gradually add the granulated sugar and mix well. Beat in the eggs until fluffy. Add the flour mixture and the milk and beat until smooth. Spread the batter over the fruit.

Bake until golden and a toothpick inserted in the center comes out clean, 35 to 40 minutes. Cool on a wire rack for 30 minutes. Invert carefully onto a cake plate, remove the pan, and serve. Makes one 8-inch cake.

"NEW ARRIVAL"

spring

MEMORIAL DAY

"Grilling and picnicking, believe it or not, are possible in the city. Growing numbers of folks are using St. Nicholas Park and Mt. Morris Park for small family gatherings and cookouts. Then there are the backyard barbecues, or for some, a quick getaway to a weekend house. In North Carolina, traditional barbecue does not call for a red sauce; vinegar does it all. Chicken done this way is refreshing and doesn't interfere with the spicier side dishes that are usually served."

menu

•

VINEGAR-MARINATED
GRILLED CHICKEN

•

RUSSET POTATO SALAD

•

GLORIA'S
THREE-BEAN SALAD

•

PAUL'S BANANA PUDDING

•

YEZESHIWAL'S
ETHIOPIAN BREAD

•

SPICED LEMONADE

•

serves 6

VINEGAR-MARINATED GRILLED CHICKEN

2 (2+1/2- to 3-pound) broiler/fryer chickens, each cut into 8 pieces

1 tablespoon kosher salt

1 tablespoon garlic powder

1 tablespoon onion powder

1 teaspoon freshly ground black pepper

1 cup vinegar

1 cup vegetable oil

1 tablespoon crushed red pepper flakes

Season the chicken with the salt, garlic powder, onion powder, and black pepper. Place in a large plastic bag. Combine the vinegar, oil, and crushed red pepper, and pour 1+1/2 cups of this mixture over the chicken, reserving 1/2 cup to baste the chicken while cooking. Marinate the chicken overnight in the refrigerator, along with the extra marinade in a separate container.

Preheat the grill. Drain the chicken and discard the marinade. Arrange the chicken on the hot grill and cook, turning pieces often and basting with the reserved marinade. Tongs are best for turning, as a fork can pierce the chicken and release its juices. Cook until the juices run clear, about 15 minutes on each side if on an open flame, 20 minutes on each side if using a closed grill. Serves 6 to 8.

RUSSET POTATO SALAD

Don't even think about barbecue without having some potato salad. If you are traveling with it, make sure that it is kept well-chilled in a cooler; if you're serving it outside on a buffet, keep it in the shade with the serving dish placed over a large bowl of crushed ice.

3 pounds russet potatoes, unpeeled and scrubbed

1+1/2 cups mayonnaise

2 tablespoons well-drained prepared horseradish

1 tablespoon celery seeds

2 tablespoons finely chopped scallions, both white and green parts

4 teaspoons dried parsley

Place the potatoes in a large pot and fill with water to cover by 2 inches. Bring to a boil, then lower to a medium simmer. Simmer partly covered until tender but slightly resistant when pierced with a fork, 25 to 30 minutes. Drain and let cool thoroughly.

Cut the unpeeled potatoes into 1-inch cubes and place in a large bowl. In a small bowl, combine the mayonnaise, horseradish, celery seeds, scallions, and 3 teaspoons of the parsley. Pour over the potatoes. Gently mix the potatoes and dressing until evenly coated. Transfer to a serving bowl, and garnish with the remaining 1 teaspoon parsley. Cover with plastic wrap, and refrigerate until ready to serve. Serves 6 to 8.

GLORIA'S THREE-BEAN SALAD

Gloria Bynum of Chicago gave this recipe to me some 30 or more years ago; and that's how long I have been making it. What is really good about it? It can keep in your refrigerator for a month. It goes well as an accompaniment for a sandwich, baked or broiled meats, or on a salad plate with tuna fish.

2 (15-ounce) cans green beans, rinsed and drained

1 (15-ounce) can waxed beans, rinsed and drained

1 (15-ounce) can red kidney or black beans, rinsed and drained

2 medium onions, cut into thin rings

1 (4-ounce) jar pimientos, drained and cut into thin strips

1+1/2 cups sugar

2 cups white vinegar

1 cup water

1/4 cup fresh lemon juice

1 teaspoon salt

1 tablespoon mustard seeds

In a large bowl, combine the green, waxed, kidney or black beans with the onions and pimientos.

In a saucepan combine the sugar, vinegar, water, lemon juice, and salt. Bring to a boil, and lower to a simmer; cook 5 minutes. Remove from heat and stir; let the mixture cool.

Add the vinegar mixture to the beans, and toss all together. Sprinkle in the mustard seeds, and gently toss again. Refrigerate in a covered plastic container for at least 24 hours before serving. Serves 6.

PAUL'S BANANA PUDDING

Just about everyone with a Southern background loves banana pudding. Everyone makes it differently—and, unfortunately, not as frequently as many would like. Anyone who makes this version will face adamant demands for more.

2 large eggs or 3 small eggs

2/3 cup sugar

1/3 cup cornstarch

2+1/2 cups milk

1 tablespoon pure vanilla extract

2 tablespoons butter

1 box vanilla wafers

4 bananas, peeled and sliced

Preheat the oven to 375°. Beat the eggs together with the sugar and cornstarch. Pour the milk into the top of a double boiler set over simmering water, and add the egg mixture to the milk, stirring constantly. Stir in the vanilla and butter until the butter is melted and all is well blended. Remove from the heat.

In a deep Pyrex dish, place a layer of vanilla wafers, then cover with a layer of bananas, then enough custard to cover. Repeat the layers ending with custard. Bake until golden brown on top, 10 to 12 minutes. Serves 6 to 8.

YEZESHIWAL'S ETHIOPIAN BREAD

In Ethiopia, when prayers are answered, a loaf of bread is baked and taken to the church for the priests. Yezeshiwal Woldeamanuel also brings it to her friends, along with other goodies. The bread is fragrant, and packed with the most interesting flavors.

1 (1/4-ounce) package active dry yeast

1 tablespoon salt

3 tablespoons brown sugar

1 teaspoon ground cardamom

2 tablespoons ajawain seeds or kalonji (available at east Indian grocery stores)

1 tablespoon baking powder

1 teaspoon baking soda

1 teaspoon freshly puréed garlic

1 teaspoon freshly puréed ginger

1/2 cup corn oil

2 pounds bread flour

3/4 cup dry white wine, at room temperature, or lukewarm water

Butter, for pan

In a large bowl, mix together the yeast, salt, brown sugar, cardamom, ajawain, baking powder, baking soda, garlic, ginger, and oil. Let stand for 15 to 20 minutes.

Sift the flour into the mixture; knead with the palms of your hands, adding wine (or water) until the dough is sticky. Knead the dough for 10 minutes.

Place the dough in a warm place and cover bowl with a flat tray until it doubles in bulk.

Grease a loaf pan with butter.

Spread the dough in the pan and set aside to rise again until the size increases by 1/3, about 5 to 7 minutes.

Preheat the oven to 200°. Place the pan in the oven and raise the temperature to 375°. Bake until golden brown, 35 to 40 minutes.

Remove the bread from the oven and let it stand for 10 minutes. Cover with paper towels, then cover tightly with aluminum foil; let the bread stand, wrapped, for 15 minutes before serving (this softens the bread). Serves 6.

SPICED LEMONADE

Some years ago at the 125th Street Mart, which is now closed, there was a vendor upstairs in the food court who made unbelievable lemonade. I've worked on this for a couple of years, and I think she would approve of the result.

1/4 to 1/2 cup sugar, to taste

2 quarts water

1 tablespoon whole cloves

7 large lemons

2 large limes

Place the sugar, water, and cloves in a large saucepan; bring to a slow boil, turn the heat down, and simmer for 10 minutes. Remove from heat and let cool.

Roll 6 of the lemons on a hard surface, cut them in half, and squeeze the juice into a measuring cup. Roll two limes, cut them in half, and squeeze the juice of 1+1/2 limes into the lemon juice. Ream the lemons and limes out with a spoon, adding the pulp to the juice. Strain the clove syrup into a large pitcher. Strain the lemon-lime juice, pressing on the pulp, into the pitcher. Slice the remaining lemon and 1/2 lime, and add the slices to the pitcher. Chill.

Serve in tall glasses filled with ice, with a slice of lemon and lime in each glass. Makes 8 cups.

spring

GRADUATION DINNER

"When my niece Rita's two beautiful daughters, Zahava and Faradiina, graduated from college, she celebrated big time. This is what she served. It isn't a celebration if you don't have a ham, and like everything else Rita does, her ham comes with imagination."

menu

•

COCA-COLA BAKED HAM

•

MUST-HAVE
MACARONI AND CHEESE

•

SIMPLE STEAMED BROCCOLI

•

PECAN PIE

•

suggested drink:
BOUVET BRUT ROSÉ

•

serves 6

COCA-COLA BAKED HAM

1 (12- to 14-pound) fully cooked bone-in ham

2 liters Coca-Cola

1 tablespoon whole cloves

1/2 cup firmly packed dark brown sugar

1/3 cup dark Karo syrup

Place the ham in a large pot. Pour enough Coca-Cola to cover the ham completely. Bring to a boil. Reduce the heat, cover partially, and simmer on low heat for 10 minutes per pound, or 2+1/2 hours total. Keep the ham in the liquid until just cool enough to handle; do not cool completely.

Preheat the oven to 350°. Drain the ham, and place it on a platter or carving board. Using a sharp knife, remove the rind from the ham, leaving a 1/4-inch layer of fat. Score the ham, creating a diamond pattern. Stick a clove into the center of each diamond. Mix the brown sugar and Karo syrup and pack the mixture all over the ham.

Place the ham on a 12x8x2-inch disposable aluminum pan and bake until brown and crisp, 25 minutes, basting with the remaining sugar and Karo syrup, thinned with a little fresh cola. When the ham is done, remove it from the oven to rest, continuing to baste every 15 minutes while it cools. Cool for 30 minutes before carving. Serves 6 to 8, with leftovers.

MUST-HAVE MACARONI AND CHEESE

1 teaspoon salt for pasta water

2 cups elbow macaroni

2 eggs, lightly beaten

1+3/4 cups evaporated milk

3 tablespoons unsalted butter, melted

1+1/2 cups grated extra-sharp cheddar cheese

1/2 cup grated Parmesan cheese

Preheat the oven to 350°. Bring a large saucepan of water to a boil; add salt. Add the macaroni and boil, uncovered, 10 minutes. While the macaroni is boiling, beat the eggs, evaporated milk, and melted butter in a bowl. Drain the macaroni and rinse it under cold water; drain.

In a greased 2-quart casserole dish, layer the macaroni and cheeses, ending with cheese on top. Pour the egg mixture over the top; bake for 30 minutes until golden brown. Serve hot. Serves 6.

SIMPLE STEAMED BROCCOLI

Every now and then you have so many flavors going on in a meal that it's refreshing to have something on the menu that has no seasoning and carries its own fresh taste. Broccoli is one vegetable that does not need additional flavoring.

2 large bunches very fresh broccoli, heavy stalks removed, cut into 6 to 8 pieces

Place the broccoli in a steamer basket set over boiling water. Steam until the broccoli is bright green and still has some crunch, 8 to 10 minutes. Serve immediately. Serves 6.

PECAN PIE

Now, how easy could this be? The real secret to a good pecan pie is the freshness of the pecans. Check the expiration date on the package. If you are like some people, you just go into your freezer and get out what you need from the five-pound box sent to you from Georgia. That's the kind of present you really want.

3 large eggs, lightly beaten

1 cup dark corn syrup

1 cup sugar

2 tablespoons unsalted butter, melted

2 teaspoons pure vanilla extract

1 cup chopped pecans

1 9-inch prepared pie shell (from the grocery freezer), thawed

12 pecan halves

Crème fraîche, for serving (optional)

Sugar, for serving (optional)

Preheat the oven to 350°. In a bowl, whisk together the eggs, corn syrup, sugar, melted butter, and vanilla. Add the chopped pecans. Pour the filling into the piecrust. Arrange the pecan halves on top of the filling. Bake until the filling is just barely set and a knife inserted in the middle comes out clean, 45 to 50 minutes. Serve at room temperature. A dollop of crème fraîche with a little sprinkle of sugar complements the sweetness of the pie. Serves 8.

spring

CHICKEN GONE FANCY

"There's a special affinity between chicken and wine—they seem to bring out the best in each other. This recipe is a good choice for company, as it can be prepared ahead and reheated. When you cook for your peers, that's one thing. When you cook for the elder members of your family—all good cooks—you'd better tap dance. My niece Kathy Lyles did just that. We were all impressed, especially with the spinach. She showed us that you can be pretty and cook, too."

menu

•

CHICKEN IN WINE SAUCE
WITH RICE

•

KATHY'S SPINACH

•

MISSISSIPPI MUD PIE

•

serves 4

CHICKEN IN WINE SAUCE WITH RICE

1 (3+1/2-pound) broiler/fryer chicken, cut into 8 pieces

1/3 cup all-purpose flour

1/4 teaspoon freshly ground black pepper

3 tablespoons corn oil

1 medium onion, finely chopped

2 cloves garlic, finely minced

1/2 cup water

1 chicken bouillon cube

1 (8-ounce) can tomato sauce

1/2 cup dry sherry

1/2 teaspoon chili powder

1/4 cup sliced stuffed green olives

1 (8-ounce) can sliced mushrooms, drained

Long-grain white rice

Rinse the chicken thoroughly; pat dry with paper towel. Wash hands and surfaces after handling chicken. Combine the flour and pepper in a shallow bowl or a bag, and coat the chicken with the flour mixture. Heat the oil in a large heavy skillet over medium heat. Add the chicken and brown slowly on all sides. Add the onion and garlic to the skillet and continue cooking until they become translucent. In a seperate saucepan, bring water to a boil and add the bouillon cube. Add the tomato sauce, sherry, bouillon mixture, chili powder, olives, and mushrooms to the skillet. Cover and simmer on a low flame for 1 hour.

Cook the rice according to package directions for 4 people. Serve the chicken over the rice or with rice on the side. Serves 4.

KATHY'S SPINACH

2 teaspoons olive oil

1 teaspoon minced garlic (available in jars)

2 teaspoons teriyaki sauce

1 (10-ounce) package prewashed spinach

1 (10-ounce) package prewashed baby spinach

Freshly ground black pepper, to taste

Heat the oil in a large skillet over medium heat. Add the garlic and teriyaki sauce, then the spinach and pepper. Sauté until spinach is just wilted, 3 to 4 minutes. Serves 4.

MISSISSIPPI MUD PIE

I remember that Mississippi was the first long word I learned how to spell as a five-year-old. To celebrate that feat, my proud mother treated me with a Mississippi mud pie. I was reluctant to eat it, because I wasn't into eating mud. Mother wasn't sure how it came by that name, and to date no one seems to know. What I do know is that if you have ever experienced this pie, it really doesn't matter: This is a chocolate lover's delight.

4 ounces semisweet chocolate

1/2 cup (1 stick) butter

3 eggs

1/4 cup light corn syrup

1 teaspoon pure almond extract

3/4 cup sugar

Pinch of salt

1 frozen (9-inch) single piecrust, thawed

Whipped cream, for serving

Preheat the oven to 350°. Melt the chocolate and butter in a double boiler over moderate heat.

In a large bowl, beat the eggs and stir in the corn syrup, almond extract, sugar, and salt. Slowly pour melted chocolate into egg mixture, stirring slowly to combine. Pour into the pie shell. Bake until the pie is just set but still soft inside, 30 to 35 minutes. Remove it from the oven and let set completely. Serve slightly warm with whipped cream on top. Makes one 9-inch pie.

spring

SPRING BREAKFAST

“If you have been around the block, you know about ham and red-eye gravy. No mystery: It's all about strong coffee in the morning, which gets the red out of your eyes, and how it ends up on your breakfast ham. If this doesn't wake you up, call in sick. Serve grits with this meal, prepared according to package directions for 6 people; this will allow ample servings for 4.”

menu

•

FRIED COUNTRY HAM
WITH RED-EYE GRAVY

•

DOLL'S FRIED APPLES

•

GRITS

•

SCRAMBLED EGGS
WITH SCALLIONS

•

AUNT LULA'S YEAST ROLLS

•

serves 4

FRIED COUNTRY HAM WITH RED-EYE GRAVY

4 (1/4-inch-thick) center-cut slices country ham, fat trimmed off and reserved

1/2 cup brewed coffee

In a heavy skillet, fry half of the reserved fat trimmings over medium-high heat until the fat is rendered. Discard the fried trimmings from the skillet.

In the same skillet, fry the ham 1 slice at a time over medium-high heat, turning once, until it is light golden brown, about 2 minutes per side. Transfer to a platter as ham is fried, and keep in a warm oven until ready to serve.

Add the remaining fat trimmings to the drippings in the skillet, and render the fat over medium-high heat, stirring and scraping up the brown bits with a fork or spatula. Discard the trimmings.

Stir the coffee into the hot skillet, a few drops at a time, and let the mixture simmer for a few minutes.

Pour a little of the gravy over each piece of ham. Transfer the remaining gravy to a sauceboat and serve on the side. Serves 4.

DOLL'S FRIED APPLES

4 tablespoons (1/2 stick) unsalted butter

4 large Red Delicious apples, cored and sliced into 1/2-inch-thick slices

3/4 cup sugar

1/2 teaspoon cinnamon

1/4 cup water

In a heavy skillet over medium heat, melt the butter; layer the apple slices in the melted butter, sprinkling the sugar and cinnamon between the layers.

Add the water, and simmer on a low flame until the apples become soft and caramelized, about 5 minutes. Remove from the pan with a slotted spatula and put on plates. Spoon any syrup from the skillet over the apples. Serve warm. Serves 4.

SCRAMBLED EGGS WITH SCALLIONS

8 large eggs

3 tablespoons half-and-half

1 teaspoon Lawrey's seasoned salt

4 tablespoons unsalted butter

2 scallions, rinsed, split, and cut into 1/2-inch dice (use all of the white part, and 1/4 of the green part)

Whisk the eggs, half-and-half, and seasoned salt together in a bowl. Melt the butter in a skillet over medium-low heat; do not let the butter brown. Add the scallions, and sauté until soft, 4 to 5 minutes. Pour the egg mixture into the skillet and scramble with a large spoon or rubber spatula until cooked. Serves 4.

AUNT LULA'S YEAST ROLLS

My friend Jackie Shropshire is bicoastal, making stops all along the way and through Harlem. She said not to forget her Aunt Lula's yeast rolls. If you have never had yeast rolls, treat yourself to these; with last summer's watermelon preserves, they are especially divine (see recipe on page 145).

3 cups all-purpose flour

1 tablespoon sugar

1 teaspoon salt

2 teaspoons baking powder

1/4 teaspoon baking soda

1 (0.6-ounce) cake compressed fresh yeast or 1 (1/4-ounce) package of active dry yeast

1/2 cup lukewarm water

5 tablespoons vegetable shortening

3 tablespoons butter

2 eggs, beaten

3/4 cup milk

Preheat the oven to 400°. Stir together the flour, sugar, salt, baking powder, and baking soda. Dissolve the yeast in the lukewarm water. In a large bowl cream the shortening, butter, and eggs together. Stir in the yeast mixture. Gradually add the milk, alternating with the flour mixture. Mix well. Cover dough and let rise in a warm place for 2 hours.

Punch the dough down and let it rise again for 45 minutes to 1 hour. Roll the dough out to 1/2-inch thickness and cut out circles using a 3-inch drinking glass. Make an indentation across 1/3 of the circle and fold the dough over to make a half-circle. Place on a baking sheet and bake until golden brown, about 15 minutes. Makes 12 rolls.

SUMMER

FOURTH OF JULY
MENU

MARINATED GRILLED BABY BACK RIBS

FIREWORKS COLESLAW

HARLEM SUMMER BEAN SALAD

DOLL'S BLACKBERRY COBBLER

see recipes page 128

summer

CHRISTINA'S WORLD

"Christina Figueras Colon is the daughter I never had, and the cook that I would love to be. Having been raised by gourmet parents, and having been a flight attendant who has traveled the world, she brings so much excitement and surprise to what she cooks, that relatives and friends beat a path to her kitchen door."

menu

•

ESCOVITCHED KINGFISH

•

RED BEANS

•

YELLOW RICE

•

PLANTAINS CHRISTINA

•

TOMATO AND RED ONION SALAD

•

CHRISTINA'S MANGO MOUSSE

•

suggested drink:
CORONA BEER

•

serves 6

ESCOVITCHED KINGFISH

One of the mysteries of soul food is how, from Dakar, Senegal to Harlem to Wilmington, North Carolina, kingfish is cooked the same way. When I was visiting my family in Wilmington, North Carolina, my nephew Tony came home with a large kingfish that I immediately started to clean and cut into steaks. It was going to be a quick trip to Africa and Jamaica that night. Mystery number two: Did Tony really catch that fish, or did he buy it off someone else's line?

6 (1/2-inch-thick) kingfish steaks

1/2 teaspoon salt

1 teaspoon freshly ground black pepper

Juice of 1 lime

1/2 cup plus 2 tablespoons corn oil

1 large Bermuda onion, cut in half and thinly sliced

2 green bell peppers, sliced into thin rings

2 red bell peppers, sliced into thin rings

1 small Scotch bonnet pepper, thinly sliced (see Note)

1/2 cup white wine vinegar

Season the fish steaks with the salt, pepper, and lime juice, and set aside. In a medium skillet, heat 2 tablespoons of the oil over medium heat, and lower to a simmer. Add the onion, bell peppers, and Scotch bonnet pepper; cover and cook for 5 minutes, then add the vinegar and cook for an additional 5 minutes. Remove from heat, remove the lid, and set aside.

In another medium skillet, heat 1/4 cup of the oil over medium heat until quite hot but not smoking. Add the fish steaks 2 at a time, and fry until golden and crispy, about 2 minutes on each side; drain on paper towels, and continue to fry the rest of the fish this way, adding more oil as necessary.

Arrange the fish on a platter, and top with the pickled onions and peppers. Serves 6.

Note: Wash hands immediately after handling these very hot peppers and avoid contact with your eyes and skin.

RED BEANS

Do we love red beans and rice in Harlem! They're always to be found on the menu in Latino restaurants.

1 pound dried kidney beans

1 ham hock

1 tablespoon olive oil

1 medium onion, chopped

1 small green pepper, chopped

2 cloves garlic, minced

1 bay leaf

1 teaspoon dried thyme

1/2 teaspoon ground cumin

1/2 teaspoon crushed red pepper flakes

1/2 teaspoon salt

1/2 teaspoon freshly ground black pepper

1 teaspoon sugar

Rinse the beans, and soak in 4 cups cold water overnight.

Put the ham hock in a large pot with enough water to cover and simmer until soft, about 2 hours. Remove the ham from the liquid, reserving both the ham hock and the liquid.

Heat the olive oil in a large skillet over medium heat, and sauté the onion, green pepper, and garlic until semi-opaque but not too soft, about 5 minutes.

Drain and rinse the soaked beans, and place them in a 6-quart pot. Add 4 cups of the liquid from the ham hock. Add the sautéed onion, green pepper, and garlic to the pot, along with the bay leaf, thyme, cumin, crushed red pepper, salt, black pepper, and sugar. Bring to a boil, and immediately lower to a simmer. Cover the pot and simmer for 1 hour. Cut the meat from the ham hock and add to the pot, and allow to cook for another 30 minutes. Serve with yellow rice on the side; see recipe on page 106. Serves 6.

VARIATION: Instead of the ham hock, you can substitute 1 tablespoon corn oil and a few dashes of Liquid Smoke. For the ham hock liquid, use 4 cups water and a little liquid smoke.

CHRISTINA'S YELLOW RICE

3 tablespoons olive oil

3 tablespoons sofrito, such as Goya brand

1 (8 ounce) can tomato sauce

2 teaspoons salt

3 cups long-grain rice

In a heavy medium saucepan set over high heat, heat the olive oil. Stir in the sofrito, tomato sauce, and salt. When mixture comes to a boil, add the rice and stir to combine. Add 3 cups water, cover, and reduce heat to medium. Cook until water is absorbed, about 30 minutes. Serves 6.

PLANTAINS CHRISTINA

6 ripe (black-skinned) but firm plantains

1 cup orange juice

1/4 Grand Marnier or other orange-flavored liqueur (optional)

4 cloves

1/2 cup firmly packed light brown sugar

2 or 3 lemon peel curls

Preheat the oven to 325°. Peel the plantains and slice them in half lengthwise, or make 2-inch-long slices cutting on the diagonal, and place them in a 8x8-inch square or oval Pyrex baking dish. Add the orange juice, Grand Marnier or other orange-flavored liqueur, cloves, brown sugar, and lemon peels, and cover the dish with aluminum foil. Bake until the plantains have absorbed some of the liquid and are soft, about 15 minutes. Lift with a slotted spoon onto a serving plate, and spoon some of the liquid over them. Serves 6.

TOMATO AND RED ONION SALAD

3 to 4 large tomatoes, sliced thin

1 large red onion, sliced thin

2 tablespoons olive oil

1 tablespoon vinegar

Goya adobo, to taste

Alternate slices of tomato and thin slices of onion on a salad plate; sprinkle with oil, vinegar, and Goya adobo. Serves 6.

CHRISTINA'S MANGO MOUSSE

5 large, ripe mangoes, peeled

2+1/2 tablespoons unflavored powdered gelatin

7 ounces sweetened condensed milk

2 cups heavy cream

2 cups sugar

Cut 4 of the mangoes into medium-size pieces. Purée in a blender until smooth; strain through a fine-mesh sieve. Place 1/2 cup mango purée and the gelatin in a saucepan over low heat, and stir until the gelatin dissolves; remove from heat.

In a large bowl, combine both purées and the condensed milk.
Refrigerate for about 15 minutes.

In another large bowl, use an electric mixer to whip the cream with the sugar until stiff. Remove the mango mixture from the refrigerator and fold in the whipped cream. Pour into 6 dessert glasses, and refrigerate for 1 hour before serving.

Dice the remaining mango and use to garnish the desserts. Serves 6.

summer

PORK CHOP PASSION

"The ancient oral tradition of passing down our history includes how we do everyday things. For instance, a neighborhood lady, Mrs. Viola Adams from Guyana, once casually mentioned that her mother soaked her pork chops in vinegar and garlic before frying. That was enough for me. I have a passion for pork chops and garlic, and for the past decades (I won't say how many), I have been preparing this dish, to the delight of my family and friends, and it is with rare exception that I do not think of Mrs. Adams when I make it."

menu

•

MRS. ADAMS'S PICKLED PORK CHOPS

•

SOUTHERN MASHED POTATOES

•

OKRA AND TOMATOES

•

DOT'S COFFEE MOUSSE

•

suggested drink:
CALIFORNIA CHABLIS

•

serves 4

MRS. ADAMS'S PICKLED PORK CHOPS

8 thin-sliced (1/4-inch) loin pork chops

1/3 cup apple cider vinegar

1 tablespoon garlic powder

1 tablespoon onion powder

1/4 cup corn oil

1/2 cup all-purpose flour

1 teaspoon salt

1/2 teaspoon cayenne pepper

1/2 teaspoon curry powder

In a glass pan, soak the chops in the vinegar, garlic powder, and onion powder overnight in the refrigerator, turning once or twice.

Heat the oil in a large skillet over medium heat until hot but not smoking. Mix the flour with the salt, cayenne pepper, and curry powder in a plastic bag. Add 4 chops at a time to the bag, and coat evenly; shake off excess flour. Place 3 or 4 chops at a time in the hot oil; do not crowd the pan. Fry for 5 minutes on each side. Remove and serve. Serves 4.

SOUTHERN MASHED POTATOES

4 cups water

1 medium onion

5 medium russet potatoes, cut into large cubes

Unsalted butter, to taste

Salt and freshly ground black pepper, to taste

In a 2-quart saucepan, bring water to a boil, and lower to a simmer. Cut the onion in half, and slice each half crosswise into thick slices; add to the water and simmer for 15 minutes. Add the potatoes and simmer partly covered until soft, about 25 minutes. Drain, and mash with butter, salt, and pepper. Serve immediately. Serves 4.

OKRA AND TOMATOES

Okra came to this country from Africa, where it is pronounced "okro." In South Carolina, it is cooked the same way as in Africa—to a mucilaginous consistency. To say that this is overcooked is not correct—that is the traditional way of cooking okra. My preference is for crisper okra, but both ways are wonderful.

1 tablespoon extra-virgin olive oil

1 small onion, chopped

2 cloves garlic, finely minced

1 (15+1/2-ounce) can diced tomatoes, drained

1 teaspoon sugar

1/2 teaspoon dried oregano

1 or 2 dashes hot sauce, such as Tabasco

1 pound small okra, stems trimmed, sliced into 1/3-inch pieces

Heat the oil in a large skillet over medium heat, and sauté the onion and garlic until translucent, about 5 minutes. Add the tomatoes, sugar, oregano, and hot sauce, and simmer for 10 minutes. Add the okra and simmer to the desired consistency, about 20 minutes for crisper, 25 minutes for softer. Serves 4.

DOT'S COFFEE MOUSSE

My good friend Dorothy (Dot) Vaughn loves her coffee so much that she'll whip up a coffee dessert for a guest in record time.

4 eggs, separated

1/2 cup sugar

1/2 cup strong brewed coffee

2 tablespoons Kahlúa or other coffee-flavored liqueur

2 teaspoons unflavored powdered gelatin

Whipped cream, for serving

Beat the egg yolks and sugar with an electric mixer in a medium bowl until pale and fluffy, about 3 minutes. Mix the coffee and Kahlúa or other coffee-flavored liqueur in a small saucepan, and sprinkle with the gelatin. Set aside until the gelatin softens, 5 to 8 minutes. Cook the coffee mixture over medium heat, stirring constantly, just until the gelatin completely dissolves. Stir the coffee mixture into the egg yolks. Let cool to room temperature, and then refrigerate.

Clean and dry the mixers, and beat the egg whites in a separate bowl until they are stiff but not dry. Fold them into the coffee mixture. Spoon into individual dessert glasses, and chill. Top with a dollop of whipped cream to serve. Serves 4 to 6.

summer

BROWNSTONE DINING

“Donald Coaxum Marquez, who shows his home yearly at the Mt. Morris Park Historical Home Tour, knows a thing or two about houses. He is a real estate developer who also knows his way around a kitchen—a detail man who doesn't get involved unless he is sure that the end result will be spectacular. Case in point: his colorful fish dish accompanied by his impressive-looking and tasty, all-green salad, complete with a green dressing. Then, to cool down all of the heat and spice of this meal, custard is the perfect choice for dessert. Christina makes a mean tembleque, which is the Puerto Rican version of the classic Spanish flan.”

menu

•

RED SNAPPER MT. MORRIS PARK
WITH RICE

•

GREEN SALAD
WITH AVOCADO VINAIGRETTE

•

TEMBLEQUE

•

serves 4

RED SNAPPER MT. MORRIS PARK WITH RICE

2 cloves garlic

1/2 teaspoon salt

1/2 cup fresh lime juice

1 (3+1/2- to 4-pound) whole red snapper, with the head on, cleaned

Olive oil, for baking dish

Fresh flat-leaf parsley, for garnish

SAUCE

1/3 cup olive oil

1+1/2 cups chopped onion

1+1/2 tablespoons minced garlic

3 bay leaves

1+1/2 teaspoons dried oregano, crumbled

1 teaspoon dried thyme

Salt and freshly ground pepper, to taste

2 (28-ounce) cans Italian plum tomatoes, with juice, chopped

1/4 cup chopped fresh flat-leaf parsley

Long-grain white rice

Prepare the fish: Mince the garlic, and mash it with salt, forming a paste. Place the garlic paste in a bowl and combine with the lime juice. With a sharp knife, poke holes in each side of the red snapper in several places. Put the snapper in a large shallow dish, and pour the lime juice mixture inside the cavity and over the snapper. Let the snapper marinate, covered, in the refrigerator, turning once, for at least 2 hours.

Meanwhile, make the sauce: Heat the oil in a heavy skillet over medium heat and cook the onion, garlic, bay leaves, oregano, thyme, salt, and pepper, stirring, until the onion is soft and pale golden, 10 to 15 minutes. Stir in the tomatoes and their juices. Bring the mixture to a boil, and then lower to a simmer and cook, stirring occasionally, until the sauce is very thick and reduced to about 5 cups, 1 to 1+1/2 hours. Stir in the parsley and discard the bay leaves.

Preheat the oven to 350°. Lightly oil a baking dish with olive oil. Transfer the snapper using a wide spatula (or 2 spatulas) to the baking dish. Spoon about half of the sauce over the fish, cover the remaining sauce and keep warm. Cover the baking dish with aluminum foil and bake the snapper in the middle of the oven until it just flakes when tested with a fork, 50 to 60 minutes.

While the fish is baking, prepare the rice according to package directions for 4 people.

When the fish appears done, transfer it carefully to a large platter, and spoon some of the sauce around it. Garnish the snapper with parsley, and serve the remaining sauce in a gravy boat, to pour over the rice. Serves 4.

GREEN SALAD WITH AVOCADO VINAIGRETTE

6 cups escarole, rinsed and broken into bite-size pieces

1/2 cup sliced Vidalia onion

VINAIGRETTE

1 ripe Hass avocado, pitted, peeled, and cut into chunks

1/3 cup fresh lime juice

1/4 red onion, chopped

1 tablespoon wasabi paste (available at Asian markets or specialty shops)

1 tablespoon sugar

Salt and freshly ground black pepper, to taste

1 cup extra-virgin olive oil

Toss the escarole and the onion in a large salad bowl.

Make the vinaigrette: Place the avocado, lime juice, red onion, wasabi paste, sugar, salt, and pepper in a blender and purée until smooth. With the blender running, add the oil a little at a time until emulsified.

Drizzle about 1/2 cup of vinaigrette over the salad a little at a time, tossing together until the leaves are coated. Reserve and refrigerate the rest of the dressing for another day. The lime juice will keep the avocado green for a couple of days. Serves 4.

TEMBLEQUE

1 cup milk

1+1/4 cups plus 6 tablespoons sugar

8 eggs

1 teaspoon pure vanilla extract

Preheat the oven to 350°. Pour the milk into a large saucepan. Heat until it just begins to boil. Remove from heat and add 1+1/4 cups sugar, stirring until the sugar is dissolved.

In a large bowl, beat the eggs until frothy, then gradually stir in the milk mixture. Add the vanilla and stir well.

Melt the remaining 6 tablespoons sugar in a small skillet over medium heat until light golden and caramelized. Carefully pour caramel into a 6-cup tube pan. Holding the pan with oven mitts, tilt until caramel coats the pan. Pour the egg mixture into the tube pan, then place the pan in a shallow pan filled halfway with hot water. Bake until a knife inserted in the center of the custard comes out clean, about 1 hour. Allow to cool, then let chill in the refrigerator thoroughly.

To serve run a sharp knife around inside edges of tube pan and gently invert the custard onto a serving plate. Cut the tembleque, and place slices on individual dessert plates. Serves 4 to 6.

summer

ANCESTORS' GIFT

"Elaine Calloway, born in New Orleans and raised in Harlem, does gumbo like nobody else. Watching her prepare the dish you realize that this is clearly a lot of work, but worth the effort. The word gumbo is derived from the Bantu word ngombo, for okra pods. Our enslaved ancestors brought okra to America during the Middle Passage. This may be why we have such an affinity for okra today."

menu

•

ELAINE'S CREOLE GUMBO
WITH RICE

•

SPINACH SALAD
WITH FRENCH-CREOLE DRESSING

•

ELAINE'S NEW ORLEANS
BREAD PUDDING

•

suggestd drink:
LOUIS JADOT
BEAUJOLAIS-VILLAGES 2003

•

serves 8

ELAINE'S CREOLE GUMBO WITH RICE

2 dozen blue crabs

3 pounds raw shrimp with shells on

1 carrot, peeled

3 cups finely chopped onions, plus 1 onion, quartered

1+1/2 cups finely chopped celery

1+1/4 cup vegetable oil, plus 1 tablespoon

1 cup finely chopped green bell pepper

3 cloves garlic, finely chopped

3 pounds fresh or frozen okra, cut into 1/4-inch pieces

4 andouille sausages or smoked hot beef or pork sausage, cut into 1-inch pieces

2 tablespoons all-purpose flour

1 (16-ounce) can whole tomatoes, well drained

1 teaspoon dried thyme

1 teaspoon dried basil

3 bay leaves

1 tablespoon Tabasco sauce

1 tablespoon Worcestershire sauce

1/4 cup chopped fresh flat-leaf parsley

Salt and freshly ground black pepper, to taste

1 cup long-grain white rice

Make the stock: Fill a large pot with about 8 quarts water; bring the water to a boil over high heat. Wash the crabs then place them in the boiling water; boil the crabs 5 minutes. Remove the crabs from the pot; leave water boiling. When the crabs are cool enough to handle, pull off the back shells, discard the spongy fingers, and return the back shells to the pot. Reduce the heat and simmer. Break the crab bodies in half and reserve.

Peel the shrimp, and clean them. Put the shells into the pot, reserving the raw, peeled shrimp.

Add 1 carrot, the quartered onion, and 1/2 cup of the chopped celery to the pot. Simmer, covered, for 2 hours.

Strain the stock and return it to the pot. Boil the stock, uncovered, over high heat until reduced to about 4 quarts, about 20 minutes.

Make the gumbo: Heat 1/4 cup oil in a medium skillet. Sauté 3 cups finely chopped onions, the remaining 1 cup chopped celery, the green pepper, and garlic until soft.

In a large skillet, heat 3/4 cup oil over medium heat and fry the okra until soft, stirring often. More oil can be added if the okra sticks. Add the fried okra to the onion mixture.

In a separate skillet, heat the remaining 1/4 cup oil and brown the sausage; remove from the skillet, set the sausage aside, and wipe out the skillet.

In the cleaned skillet, make a brown roux: Heat 1 tablespoon oil, and add the flour. Cook over medium heat, stirring until the mixture turns a rich brown. Stir in the tomatoes, breaking them with a wooden spoon to form a paste. Return the sausage to the skillet, add thyme, basil, and bay leaves. Sauté for 5 minutes.

Add the okra and sautéed onion mixture to the stock, then slowly stir in the sausage, tomatoes, Tabasco, and Worcestershire. Bring to a boil, and simmer for 1 hour.

Add the shrimp, crab halves, and parsley. Cover with a tight-fitting lid bring gumbo back to a boil and cook until shrimp are done, about 20 minutes. Remove bay leaves and season with salt and pepper.

Prepare the rice according to the package directions.

Place 1/4 cup cooked rice in each of 8 bowls. Ladle the gumbo over the rice. Leftovers can be frozen. Serves 8.

SPINACH SALAD WITH FRENCH-CREOLE DRESSING

2 (10-ounce) packages prewashed baby spinach

1 medium red onion, chopped

DRESSING

1/4 cup tarragon vinegar

4 teaspoons prepared Creole mustard or Dijon mustard

1 teaspoon Worcestershire sauce

2 teaspoons salt

1/2 teaspoon freshly ground black pepper

3/4 cup extra-virgin olive oil

In a large salad bowl toss the spinach with the onion.

Make the dressing: In a blender, combine the vinegar, mustard, Worcestershire, salt, and pepper. With the blender running, add the oil in small quantities until it is incorporated and emulsified.

Drizzle the dressing over the salad, using only what is needed to coat the spinach. Reserve and refrigerate the remaining dressing in a covered jar for future use.
Serves 8.

ELAINE'S NEW ORLEANS BREAD PUDDING

Now, if you think you've had it all with Elaine's gumbo, wait until she whips her bread pudding on you.

1 (10-ounce) loaf stale French bread, broken into 1-inch pieces (3 to 4 cups)

2 cups milk

1 cup sugar

4 tablespoons butter (1/2 stick), melted, plus more for the baking dish

3 eggs

1/2 tablespoon pure vanilla extract

1/2 cup raisins

1/2 cup chopped pecans

1/2 teaspoon cinnamon

1/4 teaspoon nutmeg

1 tablespoon pure vanilla extract

Preheat the oven to 350°. Butter a 13x9-inch baking dish. Combine all ingredients in a large bowl. The mixture should be moist but not soupy. Pour into the prepared dish. Place on middle rack of oven.

Bake until the top is golden brown, about 1 hour and 15 minutes. Serve warm. Serves 8.

summer

HARLEM FISH-FRY

"The Cachie, Middle, and Roanoke Rivers empty into North Carolina's Albemarle Sound. All three rivers meander through peanut country, where the legumes wash down the rivers to the mouth of the sound and into the mouths of wintering catfish. Artie Marrow and his sidekick Pablo never have to wait long to catch a cooler full of peanut-fed catfish; then they head to Harlem, for a good old-fashioned Saturday night fish-fry. This recipe doesn't call for peanut-fed catfish; any old pond-raised, river runner, or lake-pampered long-whiskers will do."

menu

•

PABLO'S FRIED CATFISH

•

TARTAR SAUCE

•

MOJO WORKIN'
CORN ON THE COB

•

ARUGULA SALAD WITH MY OWN
HOUSE DRESSING

•

NO BIG THING APPLE PIE

•

suggested drink:
BEER

•

serves 6

PABLO'S FRIED CATFISH

Vegetable oil, for frying

1 cup all-purpose flour

1 cup cornmeal

Salt, to taste

1 teaspoon freshly ground black pepper

1 teaspoon cayenne pepper (optional)

2 eggs, well beaten

6 catfish fillets

6 lemon wedges, for garnish

Tartar Sauce, for dipping (recipe follows)

Pour 1/2 inch oil into a large, heavy skillet. Heat over medium heat until hot but not smoking. In a shallow dish, thoroughly mix the flour and cornmeal, and season with salt and pepper (some cayenne is good, too, but it is optional). Place the eggs in another shallow dish. Dip the fish in the egg, then coat evenly in the cornmeal mixture. Fry in batches until golden, about 3 minutes on each side. Replace the oil if necessary as you go along. Drain on paper towels, and arrange on a platter with the lemon wedges and tartar sauce. Serves 6.

MOJO WORKIN' CORN ON THE COB

6 ears white corn, husked

6 tablespoons (3/4 stick) butter

Juice of 1/2 lime

1/2 teaspoon cayenne pepper

Salt and freshly ground black pepper, to taste

Fill a large pot with water and bring water to a boil. Drop the corn in. Simmer over medium-high heat until tender, about 8 minutes; remove corn with tongs to a flat pan.

Meanwhile, melt the butter in a small skillet over very low heat; add the lime juice and cayenne pepper, and pour the mixture over the corn, coating all sides. Season with salt and pepper.

TARTAR SAUCE

1 cup store-bought mayonnaise

1/3 cup sweet relish, drained

1/4 cup scallions, white and green parts, finely chopped

1/4 cup horseradish, drained

Combine all the ingredients in a bowl, and chill until the fish has been fried.

ARUGULA SALAD WITH MY OWN HOUSE DRESSING

Arugula has always been a popular salad green in Italy, relished for its spicy, peppery flavor. It used to be difficult to find here, but is readily available now. My salad dressing, which is slightly sweet, really jazzes it up. I beg my niece Trice to forgive me: She requested that I never give the recipe for the dressing to anyone. She said, "If all else fails, I plan to sell it." To my former husband, who has repeatedly asked for the recipe and been told that it came with the territory and not the settlement, you may now have it.

4 bunches arugula

1 cup extra-virgin olive oil

1/3 cup white wine vinegar

1 teaspoon onion powder

1 teaspoon dried parsley

3 cloves garlic, finely minced

1 teaspoon dried Italian seasoning

3 grinds black pepper

1/2 teaspoon dried dill

3-inch squeeze anchovy paste

Dash of hot sauce, such as Tabasco

2 heaping tablespoons sugar

Arugula tends to be sandy, so soak it, changing the water at least three times. Spin dry (or dry on paper towels) and trim.

Make the dressing: Place the remaining ingredients together in a blender, and blend on low speed until combined.

Place the arugula in a salad bowl and toss with about 1/4 cup dressing. Place the remaining dressing in a covered container and store in the refrigerator for later use. Serves 6.

NO BIG THING APPLE PIE

Because apple pie goes with just about everything, pleases just about everyone, and travels well, it's what you take to the fish fry. The secret to this one is to use a combination of apples.

AUNT LOU'S PIECRUST

4 cups all-purpose flour

1/8 teaspoon salt

1+1/2 cups vegetable shortening

3 tablespoons ice water

FILLING

2 Granny Smith apples, peeled, cored, and sliced

2 Red Delicious or Macintosh apples, peeled, cored, and sliced

2 tablespoons cornstarch

1 teaspoon all-purpose flour

1 teaspoon cinnamon

3 tablespoons unsalted butter, melted

1 teaspoon pure vanilla extract

1 tablespoon fresh lemon juice

Preheat the oven to 350°. Make the crust: Sift the flour and salt together. Add the shortening to the flour, and start mixing together with your fingers until it becomes fine and pebbly. Add the ice water, and form into a ball. Divide the ball in half, and roll each out into a 10"-round crust. Gently lift one circle into the bottom of a 9-inch pie pan.

Make the filling: Mix the apples with the cornstarch, flour, and cinnamon. Add the butter, vanilla, and lemon juice. Pour the filling into the pie shell. Add the top crust and pinch the edges together. Make a 1-inch cut in center of the top crust. Bake until the crust is golden and the fruit is bubbling, 35 to 40 minutes. Serves 6 to 8.

"HARLEM USA"

summer

FOURTH OF JULY

“In the backyard, in the park, in the country—on the grill, or in your oven, it’s barbecue big time. Ribs seem to signal the start of summer. Prepared with a dry rub, marinated, with lots of sauce, or eaten dry without sauce— the choice is yours. There are enough ways to cook them so that you can do your own thing, but you really should try this.”

menu

•

MARINATED GRILLED
BABY BACK RIBS

•

FIREWORKS COLESLAW

•

HARLEM SUMMER
BEAN SALAD

•

DOLL'S
BLACKBERRY COBBLER

•

serves 6 to 8

MARINATED GRILLED BABY BACK RIBS

MARINADE

1/3 cup bourbon

1/4 cup soy sauce

1/4 cup firmly packed light brown sugar

1 large onion, chopped

3 tablespoons Dijon mustard

1 tablespoon Worcestershire sauce

4 racks baby back pork ribs

Dipping sauce (see recipe below)

Marinate the ribs: Whisk together the bourbon, soy sauce, brown sugar, onions, mustard, and Worcestershire sauce. Place the ribs in a large plastic bag and pour half of the marinade over the ribs. Refrigerate overnight, turning to coat the ribs with the marinade. Reserve and refrigerate the remaining half of the marinade to baste the ribs while cooking.

If cooking on a grill: Heat the grill with all the coals off to one side. Cut the racks of marinated ribs into 4- or 6-rib sections. Grill over indirect heat (the side without the coals), covered, until the meat is tender, about 1+1/2 hours, basting frequently with the reserved marinade. Use half of the dipping sauce (see recipe below) to baste the ribs during the last 5 minutes of cooking. Serve the other half on the side.

If cooking in the oven: Preheat the oven to 350°. Place the ribs on a rack in a shallow roasting pan and bake for 1+1/2 hours, basting with the marinade, until tender. Use half of the dipping sauce (see recipe below) to baste the ribs during the last 5 minutes of cooking. Serve the other half on the side. Serves 6 to 8.

DIPPING SAUCE

1 tablespoon olive oil

1 small onion, minced

1 small green pepper, minced

1/3 cup hot sauce, such as Tabasco

2/3 cup orange juice

1/4 cup honey

1/4 cup bourbon

In a small saucepan over low heat, heat the oil. Add the onion and green pepper and sauté until soft, stirring. Add the hot pepper sauce, orange juice, honey, and bourbon, and simmer until the sauce thickens slightly, about 5 minutes. Makes about 1 cup.

FIREWORKS COLESLAW

There is no way of getting around making coleslaw to go with barbecue. The freshness and the crunch of the slaw make this the perfect pairing. The kids love it—and they don't even know they're getting their veggies.

COLESLAW

1/2 pound white cabbage, cored, quartered, and thinly sliced (about 3 cups)

1/2 pound red cabbage, cored, quartered, and thinly sliced (about 3 cups)

1 red bell pepper, thinly sliced into 1-inch-long strips

1 yellow bell pepper, thinly sliced into 1-inch-long strips

1 green bell pepper, thinly sliced into 1-inch-long strips

1 carrot, thinly sliced lengthwise with a vegetable peeler into 1-inch-long strips

2 scallions, thinly sliced

3 tablespoons fresh flat-leaf parsley leaves

DRESSING

1/4 cup vegetable oil

1/4 cup apple cider vinegar

1 tablespoon prepared horseradish, drained well

1 teaspoon celery seeds

1/2 teaspoon garlic powder

1/2 teaspoon onion powder

2 teaspoons sugar

1/4 teaspoon freshly ground black pepper

Salt, to taste

Make the coleslaw: Combine all of the ingredients in a large bowl. This can be done the day before and refrigerated in a plastic bag.

Make the dressing: Place all the ingredients in a blender and emulsify for 15 seconds. Refrigerate until ready to use.

In a large bowl, combine the shredded vegetable mixture and the dressing, tossing well to coat. Serves 8.

HARLEM SUMMER BEAN SALAD

If you talk the talk, you have to walk the walk. This is what Timothy Van Dam and Ron Wagner are all about: suave, handsome, personable, talented interior designers. Not in your face, just good neighbors who know how to go with the flow. If this weren't enough, they cook, too.

1 (16-ounce) package dried small white beans, such as navy beans

2 (12+3/4-ounce) cans chicken broth

1/4 teaspoon crushed red pepper flakes

1/2 cup olive oil

1 medium onion, chopped

3 cloves garlic, chopped

1/2 cup chopped fresh cilantro

1/2 cup chopped fresh flat-leaf parsley

1/2 cup balsamic vinegar

Salt and freshly ground black pepper, to taste

Rinse and pick over the beans. Place beans in a large pot and cover with water. Let stand at room temperature overnight.

Drain beans, discarding the water. In a large nonreactive pot (anything but aluminum), combine the beans, broth, and red pepper flakes. Bring to a boil, reduce the heat, and simmer until the beans are tender and all of the liquid is absorbed, 1 to 1+1/2 hours. Remove from heat and drain thoroughly.

In a small saucepan, heat 1/4 cup of the olive oil over medium-low heat, and sauté the onion and garlic until tender and translucent, about 5 minutes. Remove from heat.

Place the beans in a large bowl, add the onion and garlic, cilantro, and parsley. Whisk the remaining 1/4 cup oil and the vinegar together and gently toss with the beans. Season with salt and pepper. Serve at room temperature. Serves 8 to 10.

DOLL'S BLACKBERRY COBBLER

Peach cobbler is good, but blackberry cobbler is something else. Many years ago at Silvercrest, our family's guest house in the Catskills, we children would take our tin cans and go blackberry picking. Proudly, we would burst into the kitchen and present them to my mother, Doll. We didn't ask her to make anything with them, because we knew that the berries would be turned into a cobbler or a pie that day.

6 tablespoons unsalted butter, melted, plus more for the pan

1 cup sugar

1 cup all-purpose flour

2 teaspoons baking powder

1/4 teaspoon salt

1/2 cup milk

6 cups blackberries

1 cup apple juice

Preheat the oven to 375°. Butter a 2-quart casserole. In a medium bowl beat together 6 tablespoons butter and 1/2 cup of the sugar. In a separate bowl, stir together the flour, baking powder, and salt. Stir the flour mixture into the butter mixture, alternating with the milk, stirring until combined. Turn the dough into the prepared casserole. Top with the blackberries and sprinkle with the remaining 1/2 cup sugar. Heat the apple juice to a boil and pour it over the berries. Bake until the berries are bubbling and the top is browned, about 50 minutes. Serves 6 to 8.

summer

WHO'S FRYING CHICKEN NOW?

"Everyone's mother or grandmother made the best fried chicken, and you don't dare challenge that. I know that mine did, and yours did too, so we leave that alone. This is the code. We are talking here about Southern fried chicken—is there any other kind? I just can't do it like my mother, and I have tried, so I just get something a little more complex going on, and hope she would think that nobody can fry chicken like her daughter."

menu

•

DAUGHTER'S SOUTHERN FRIED CHICKEN

•

FRIED CORN AND SWEET PEPPERS

•

STEAMED CABBAGE WEDGES

•

BERRY DUMP CAKE

•

serves 6

DAUGHTER'S SOUTHERN FRIED CHICKEN

2 (3-pound) broiler/fryer chickens cut into 8 pieces each

1+1/2 cups all-purpose flour

1 tablespoon salt

I teaspoon freshly ground black pepper

1 tablespoon garlic powder

1 tablespoon onion powder

1 tablespoon paprika

2 teaspoons curry powder

1 teaspoon cayenne pepper

2 cups canola oil

Rinse the chickens and pat them dry with paper towels. Wash your hands and counter top thoroughly, too. Combine the flour, salt, pepper, garlic powder, onion powder, paprika, curry powder, and cayenne in a large plastic bag. Heat 1 cup of oil in each of 2 large cast-iron skillets over medium-high heat until hot but not smoking (if you don't have any, run out and get 2 seasoned ones from the Salvation Army or a thrift shop).

Shake up the chicken in the seasoned flour, and shake off any excess. Submerge the dark meat pieces in one pan of sizzling oil, and turn the heat down to medium. Fry, turning once with tongs, until golden tan, about 20 minutes on each side. Submerge the white meat in the other pan, turn the heat down to medium. Fry turning once with tongs, until golden tan, about 15 minutes on each side.

As the chicken is cooked, place on paper towels to remove excess oil and to cool slightly before serving.

NOTE: The smaller the chicken, the more tender it is when fried, so avoid buying larger ones, if you can. Adjust your cooking time for the weight of the chicken. Fry with a constant medium flame. The oil temperature should be maintained at around 350°.
Serves 6.

FRIED CORN AND SWEET PEPPERS

There is nothing as good as fresh summer corn. It can be grilled on the cob, microwaved, or boiled, but once you have had it fried (downtown they would say sautéed), you will always want it this way. It is as Southern as you can get. If you say fried corn in Harlem, everyone knows exactly what you mean.

1/4 cup bacon drippings, butter, or margarine

1 medium onion, diced

1 medium green bell pepper, seeded and diced

1 medium red bell pepper, seeded and diced

4 cups corn kernels, cut from 8 ears

4 plum tomatoes, seeded and chopped

Salt and freshly ground black pepper, to taste

In a medium skillet, melt the bacon drippings. Add the onion and peppers and cook, stirring frequently, until translucent and soft. Add the corn, tomatoes, salt, and pepper. Cook, covered, over low heat, 5 to 8 minutes. Serves 6.

STEAMED CABBAGE WEDGES

With the spicy chicken, the blandness of steamed cabbage is refreshing. And with so much going on in the kitchen, this is easy to prepare.

1/2 cup water

1 small head of cabbage with darker green outer leaves removed, rinsed, cut into wedges, and cored

Salt and freshly ground black pepper, to taste

Pour the water into a wide-bottomed saucepan; place the cabbage wedges in the pan neatly, so that the wedges all touch the bottom and are intact. Bring the water to a boil, and immediately turn down to a medium simmer. Sprinkle salt and a few grinds of pepper over the cabbage. Cover and steam until soft, 12 to 15 minutes. Remove from the pan with a large slotted spoon and put on plates. Serves 6.

BERRY DUMP CAKE

My much loved, drop-dead gorgeous nieces Trice and Michelle have dumped a lot on me over the years: their joys and woes, their kids—I even expect their pets one day. They are both "foodies" of a sort, and we spend much time talking about who is cooking what. Did I mention that they are in North Carolina, and these conversations run up our telephone bills? I should dump my bills on them. The most recent thing they dumped on me was a recipe for a cake. I kept calling them, because I thought surely they had left something out. But I just went on and tried it, and—surprise, surprise—they didn't; I am in love with this cake.

1 pint blueberries

1/2 pint blackberries

1/2 pint raspberries

3/4 cup sugar

1 box (18.25 ounces) vanilla cake mix

1 cup chopped pecans

1/2 cup (1 stick) unsalted butter, melted

Vanilla ice cream, for serving

Preheat the oven to 325°. Quickly rinse the berries and dump them into a 13x9-inch baking pan, spreading them out evenly on the bottom of the pan. Sprinkle the sugar over the berries, and then the sprinkle the dry cake mix, followed by the chopped nuts. Pour the melted butter over the nuts. Bake until the berries bubble and the topping is brown, about 1 hour. Serve warm, with a little vanilla ice cream on top. Serves 6 to 8.

"BLUES OVER HARLEM"

summer

BREAKFAST AT SILVERCREST

"Aunt Lucille was traveling upstate to visit my mother's bed and breakfast, Silvercrest. Mother had asked her to bring salt cod fish, as her guests had requested her famous cod fish cakes. Aunt Lucille boarded the unair-conditioned bus and stowed the fish in the luggage rack. Well, dried cod can be really smelly! About 1 hour out of New York City, the driver pulled into the Red Apple Rest and walked up and down the aisle until he located the offensive package. Nobody claimed it so he put it below the bus in the luggage compartment. On arrival four hours later, my aunt waited with the other passengers to collect her luggage; but when she saw the package with the fish, she decided that someone in Oneonta, which was the last stop, would be pleased to have it. Here is the meal the guests didn't get..."

menu

•

DOLL'S COD FISH CAKES

•

CHARLOTTE DOBSON'S GRITS

•

SOUTHERN
BUTTERMILK BISCUITS

•

PAUL'S WATERMELON RIND
PRESERVES

•

suggested drink:
BLOODY MARYS

•

serves 4

DOLL'S COD FISH CAKES

1 pound bacalao (dried salt cod)

4 cups water

1 small onion, thinly sliced

3 bay leaves

6 peppercorns

1 pound russet potatoes, peeled and cut into large chunks

2 large eggs

Salt and freshly ground black pepper, to taste

1/2 cup canola oil or corn oil

Cut the cod into 2-inch chunks, then place the chunks in a sieve and run cold water over them for a few minutes. Then place the cod in a bowl, cover with water, cover the bowl with plastic wrap, and refrigerate for 24 hours. At least 4 times during this period, pour off the water and replace with fresh water. The cod will freshen and plump up; it will also have a fresher smell.

Poach the fish: Pour 2 cups of the water into a 2-quart pot and add the onions, bay leaves, and peppercorns; bring to a simmer. After 5 minutes add the cod and the remaining 2 cups water. The water should cover the fish by a 1/2 inch. When it comes back to a simmer, cover immediately, and remove from the heat. Let stand for about 10 minutes, then refrigerate in its cooking liquid until thoroughly chilled. It will keep for up to one day at this point. Remove the bay leaves and peppercorns.

Place the potatoes in a large pot and cover with 2 inches of cold water; add salt. Bring to a boil over medium heat and cook until the potatoes are soft, about 15 to 20 minutes. Drain well and mash with a masher. The potatoes should be firm, not watery.

Drain the fish and place it in a bowl. Use a fork to flake it (although mother used her fingers); remove any tiny bones. Beat in the mashed potatoes with a fork. In a small bowl beat the eggs and a pinch of salt; beat 3/4 of the beaten eggs into the fish and potatoes. Mix in salt and pepper. Cover and refrigerate for 1 hour (it's easier to form the cakes when the mixture is quite cold).

Preheat the oven to 200° (or warm). Line a baking pan with paper towels. In a large frying pan, heat the oil until hot but not smoking. Use a large serving spoon to scoop up enough of the cod mixture to form a 2x3-inch fish cake. Use a rubber spatula to push the fish cake off the spoon into the oil. Fry 3 or 4 cakes at a time; do not crowd them. Fry until golden brown, 2 to 3 minutes, then turn and fry the other side until brown. Remove the fish cakes to the prepared pan and place in the oven while you fry the rest. Serve immediately. Serves 4. Makes 8 fish cakes.

CHARLOTTE DOBSON'S GRITS

Only I could marry a man so much like my father in so many ways: both from the South, and both auction fanatics who bid on everything from surprise boxes to fishing trawlers. My father had a Singer sewing machine. My husband brought to the marriage the exact same model Singer sewing machine—both men were craftsmen. Each was a fairly good cook and quite capable of fixing his own grits. What I learned from them was never serve just one portion to a grits lover, as they require two or three, and don't let them be soupy. Even if your roots are in the South, where everyone eats grits, you probably never questioned where grits come from. It doesn't grow on a tree. Hominy grits are made from dried corn that has been processed with a weak solution of lye and then hulled, resulting in a white cornmeal. Although my family always prepares them simply, by boiling, then adding butter, salt, and pepper, grits can be baked, fried, souffléd, or eaten cold as grit cakes. Charlotte Dobson, a New Yorker who has retired and now lives in Florida, has discovered grits, and likes them this way.

1 tablespoon unsalted butter

1 large onion, minced

8 slices bacon, sliced into small pieces (optional)

6 cups water

1+1/2 cups quick grits

12 ounces sharp cheddar cheese, shredded (about 3 cups)

Dash of paprika

Dash of garlic powder

Dash of white pepper

In a small skillet, melt the butter. Sauté the onion until translucent. Add the bacon and fry until crisp. Place on a plate covered with a paper towel to drain. In a large pot, bring the water to a boil. Reduce the heat to a simmer and slowly stir in the grits. Cook, stirring frequently to prevent lumps, until the grits become smooth. Add the cheese and mix well; cook until the cheese melts. Stir in the paprika, garlic powder, white pepper, bacon, and onion. Serve immediately. Serves 4 to 6.

SOUTHERN BUTTERMILK BISCUITS

I can still see my mother's long brown fingers making these. She would laugh and talk and work. It all seemed so easy—and for her it was. The biscuits were always flaky, crisp, moist, and sinfully delicious.

2 cups unbleached all-purpose flour, plus more for dusting and hands

2 teaspoons baking powder

1/2 teaspoon salt

1/3 cup half unsalted butter and half vegetable shortening, chilled

1+1/2 cups buttermilk

3/4 teaspoon baking soda

2 tablespoons heavy cream

Preheat the oven to 450° with the rack in the center. Grease two baking sheets.

Stir together the flour, baking powder, and salt in a large bowl. Use 2 knives to cut in the butter and shortening until the mixture has the texture of coarse meal. In a medium bowl, stir together the buttermilk and baking soda. Stir this mixture into the flour mixture with a big wooden spoon, just until blended; it should be slightly sticky.

Turn the dough out onto a lightly floured surface and, working quickly and gently with floured hands, pat and turn the dough about 10 times, just so it is no longer sticky. Pat the dough to a 1/2-inch thickness. Use a floured 2+1/2-inch biscuit cutter or inverted glass to cut out the biscuits, cutting them as close together as possible. Put the biscuits on the greased baking sheets, leaving at least 1 inch of space around them. Press together the unused dough and repeat. Brush the biscuit tops with a little cream.

Bake on the center rack, one sheet at a time, until the biscuits have risen and are lightly browned, 12 to 15 minutes. Makes about 18 biscuits.

PAUL'S WATERMELON RIND PRESERVES

You go Paul Evans Jr.! We know that you have been chomping at the bit to get your hands on a watermelon. No doubt you are down to the last jar of preserves in your stash that you put up last summer. You are known to share, but the last jar—never. Plead no more everyone—you can make your own. This is a divine spread on a yeast roll (see recipe on page 99) or as a glaze mixed with mustard on an oven-baked corned beef brisket. Can these in pint jars, and save one for me.

1 medium watermelon (will yield 6 pounds watermelon rind)

4 pounds sugar

1 lemon, thinly sliced

1/2 teaspoon whole cloves

1/4 cup Grand Marnier or other orange flavored liqueur (optional)

Peel off the tough green skin and cut open the watermelon and scoop out most of the fruit, leaving a little red fruit on. Cut the rind into 1-inch cubes. Place the rind in a 6-quart pot. Add the sugar, stirring it gently through the rind cubes. Set aside, at room temperature and covered with plastic wrap, for 8 to 10 hours.

Add the lemon slices and cloves, and simmer uncovered over low heat until the rind becomes translucent, 4 to 6 hours. Stir gently from time to time. Fill a glass with chilled water and drizzle a few drops of the preserve liquid into the glass. The drops should fall toward the bottom, remaining partially intact and not mixing with the syrup. This indicates that the preserves are cooked and ready to can. Stir in the optional Grand Marnier or other orange flavored liqueur.

Pack the watermelon rind and liquid into pint-sized hot sterilized canning jars, using the guidelines below.

Tips on sterilizing jars: Canning jars should be made of glass and free of any chips or cracks. Lids are made of glass, plastic, or metal (which has a rubber seal).

Boil jars and lids in a large pot of water (water level should cover jars by 1 inch) for 15 minutes. Using sterilized tongs (dip the ends in boiling water for a few minutes), remove jars and lids one by one to fill with preserves, leaving remaining equipment in the hot water. Ladle hot preserves into the hot, sterilized jars, leaving 1/4-inch space between the top of the jam and the bottom of the lid. Wipe rim of jar with a clean, damp cloth and immediately place a hot lid on top and fasten firmly. As each jar is filled and capped, place it back into the pot of hot water. When the pot is full, bring the water back to a steady boil and process for 5 minutes.

Makes about 4 quarts (or 8 pint-sized jars).

AUTUMN

COD FISH LOOKIN' GOOD
MENU

CARIBBEAN COD FISH AND PEPPERS

YELLOW RICE

WATERCRESS SALAD

LIME PIE

see recipes page 164

autumn

BABA PAUL IN THE KITCHEN

“There are some men who fish, hunt, and cook; these are but a few of Paul’s many talents. Being a Tar Heel, he would use only vinegar to barbecue, with amazing results.”

menu

•

NORTH CAROLINA BARBECUED TURKEY WINGS

•

CONFETTI CABBAGE

•

SWEET POTATO SURPRISE

•

LEMON PUDDING

•

suggested drink:
ICED TEA WITH FRESH MINT

•

serves 4

NORTH CAROLINA BARBECUED TURKEY WINGS

6 turkey wings, thawed if frozen

1 teaspoon salt

1 teaspoon freshly ground black pepper

1 teaspoon garlic powder

1 teaspoon paprika

1 teaspoon poultry seasoning

1 teaspoon onion powder

5 tablespoons corn oil or canola oil

1/3 cup apple cider vinegar

1/4 teaspoon crushed red pepper flakes

Separate the wing tips from the second joint; discard the tips if you don't like them. Combine the salt, pepper, garlic powder, paprika, poultry seasoning, and onion powder in a small bowl. Use your fingers to rub the seasoning all over the turkey wings and tips (if using); cover, and refrigerate overnight.

Preheat the oven to 350°. Coat the bottom of an 15x10-inch rimmed pan with oil, and arrange the turkey wings in a single layer in the pan. Seal the pan tightly with aluminum foil and bake for 1+1/2 hours.

Carefully remove the foil. Turn the wings, douse them liberally with vinegar, and sprinkle with the crushed red pepper. Reseal with fresh aluminum foil, and bake for an additional 30 minutes.

Remove the foil. Raise the oven temperature to broil. Broil 2 minutes to slightly crisp the wings. Serves 4.

CONFETTI CABBAGE

1/4 cup corn oil or canola oil

1/2 cup sliced onion

2/3 cup sliced green, yellow, and red bell peppers

2 cups water

1 medium head of cabbage, shredded

1 tablespoon salt

1/2 teaspoon freshly ground black pepper

Warm the oil in a 6-quart pot over low heat; add the onion and peppers and sauté until soft. Add the water and the outer, darker green cabbage leaves. Bring to a low boil then bring down to a simmer; cook for 10 minutes. Add the remaining cabbage, salt, and pepper; mix it all together, stirring the peppers, onions, and green cabbage leaves up from the bottom of the pot. Bring back up to a low boil. Lower immediately to a simmer, cover, and cook until the cabbage is opaque but still retains some crispness, 8 to 10 minutes. Remove from heat and remove the top so that it does not continue to steam. Drain before serving. Serves 4.

SWEET POTATO SURPRISE

4 tablespoons (1/2 stick) unsalted butter

1/2 teaspoon ground ginger

1/2 teaspoon grated lemon zest

2 tablespoons light brown sugar

1/4 cup orange juice

4 medium sweet potatoes

Preheat the oven to 350°. In a small saucepan melt the butter over low heat. Add the ginger, lemon zest, brown sugar, and orange juice; stir to combine; set aside.

Scrub the sweet potatoes, and wrap each in aluminum foil. Bake for 1+1/2 hours. Remove the potatoes from the oven and open the foil; cut across the top of the potato, pushing in on the ends to loosen and fluff the flesh, then gently loosen a bit more with a fork, being careful not to disturb the skin. Pour the butter mixture into each potato, and mix gently with fork. This can be prepared ahead, just rewrap in fresh aluminum foil and warm in the oven. Serves 4.

LEMON PUDDING

Butter, for baking dish

2 eggs, separated

1 cup sugar

3 tablespoons all-purpose flour

1 cup milk

1/4 teaspoon salt

Juice of 1 lemon

1 teaspoon grated lemon zest

Preheat the oven to 350°. Butter a 4x8x2-inch baking dish. In a bowl, beat the egg whites with an electric mixer until stiff. In a separate bowl, beat the yolks well.

In a large bowl, combine the sugar and flour. Add the milk, yolks, salt, lemon juice, and lemon zest. Fold in the egg whites. Pour into the prepared baking dish, and set the dish in a larger pan of warm water. Bake until the pudding forms a light fluffy cake on top and a lemon sauce on the bottom, about 35 minutes. Serves 4.

autumn

LIMA BEAN SEDUCTION

“My neighbor Betty, on meeting Michael for the first time, just knew that the way to his heart was going to be through a pot of beans. The beans worked, but the marriage didn't. But he still comes around, and she still cooks those beans, and maybe some day...”

menu

•

BETTY'S LIMA BEANS
WITH RICE

•

ESCAROLE SALAD
WITH ORANGE VINAIGRETTE

•

FRESH APPLE CAKE

•

suggested drink:
MEURSAULT

•

serves 4

BETTY'S LIMA BEANS WITH RICE

Don't even think about serving lima beans to someone from the South unless you have prepared long-grain white rice as well. Try the variations below if you'd like an alternative to pork shoulder.

2 pounds smoked pork shoulder

1 pound dried large lima beans

4 cups cold water

3 large cloves garlic, minced

1/4 teaspoon crushed red pepper flakes

2 bay leaves

1 medium onion, diced

2 tablespoons salt

1/2 teaspoon freshly ground black pepper

Long-grain white rice

Place the meat in a large pot with enough water to cover, and simmer until cooked through, about 1 hour and 10 minutes. Remove the pork from the broth and let both cool to room temperature. Refrigerate the meat and broth overnight. At the same time, soak the beans overnight in 4 cups cold water.

Rinse the soaked beans; drain. Place the beans in a 6-quart pot with 4 cups of the ham broth, the garlic, red pepper flakes, bay leaves, onion, salt, and black pepper. Bring to a low boil, then lower to a simmer. Simmer until the beans are tender, about 45 minutes, stirring occasionally. Cut the pork into bite-size pieces and add to the pot; simmer for 15 minutes.

Prepare the rice according to package directions for 4 people. Serve the rice alongside beans. Serves 4.

VARIATIONS

Smoked ham hocks: Instead of smoked shoulder, simmer 4 ham hocks in enough water to cover for approximately 2 hours. Add water to the ham hock broth to make 4 cups of liquid, and use in place of ham broth above. Cut the meat from the ham hocks and add to the pot of cooked beans; simmer for 15 minutes.

Meatless: Combine 4 cups water, 1 tablespoon corn oil, and 2 or 3 dashes Liquid Smoke and use in place of ham broth.

Ham bone: Instead of smoked shoulder, simmer a ham bone in enough water to cover for approximately 40 minutes. Let cool. Add water to the ham bone broth to make 4 cups of liquid and use in place of ham broth. Cut the meat from the bone and add to the pot of cooked beans; simmer for 15 minutes.

ESCAROLE SALAD WITH ORANGE VINAIGRETTE

The slight bitterness of escarole is an excellent contrast to the rather bland taste of lima beans. Now, if you pair the escarole with this slightly sweet, tart dressing, you have seduction big time.

1/2 cup extra-virgin olive oil

1/4 cup white wine vinegar or champagne vinegar

1/4 cup orange juice

2 teaspoons grated orange zest

1 teaspoon salt

1 teaspoon freshly ground black pepper

1 pound escarole, washed and spun dry, broken into pieces

Whisk together the oil, vinegar, orange juice, orange zest, salt, and pepper. Place the escarole in a salad bowl and drizzle with 2/3 cup dressing; toss salad. Place the remaining dressing in a covered container and refrigerate for later use. Serves 4.

FRESH APPLE CAKE

From the family recipe file of Dorothy Daniel Philips.

1/2 cup (1 stick) unsalted butter, melted, plus more for pan
2 medium Red Delicious or Macintosh apples
1+1/2 cups all-purpose flour
1 cup sugar
1 teaspoon baking soda
1 teaspoon cinnamon
1/2 teaspoon nutmeg
1/2 teaspoon allspice
1/2 teaspoon salt
1 egg, beaten
1+1/2 cups raisins
1/2 cup chopped walnuts
Confectioners' sugar, for dusting

Preheat the oven to 350°. Grease an 8-inch square baking pan. Peel and core the apples. Coarsely chop and measure 1+3/4 cups into a large bowl.

Sift the flour, sugar, baking soda, cinnamon, nutmeg, allspice, and salt together in a bowl. Stir 1/2 cup melted butter and the egg into the apples. Add the flour mixture to the apples, stirring just until blended. Add the raisins and nuts. Pour into the prepared pan. Bake until a toothpick inserted into the middle comes out clean, 50 to 55 minutes. Cool for 30 minutes, then remove from pan. Cool to room temperature. Dust with confectioners' sugar.

"BLUE LADY"

autumn

AFRICAN-FRENCH-HONDURAN-JAMAICAN FUSION

"Whether you're in Stanley McIntosh and Rosalinda Cooper's Rosalee Stewart Bed and Breakfast in Grand-Bassam, Ivory Coast, or in their Harlem brownstone, you can be sure that a meal with them will be long remembered. This husband and wife team travel back and forth between New York and Paris and the Ivory Coast, selecting only the best from food and wine merchants.

If you can catch up with them in New York and are lucky enough to be invited to dinner, you are in for an experience."

menu

•

THE ROSALEE STEWART
B & B SALAD

•

GOLDEN-YELLOW BANANA
CORNBREAD

•

PEAR PIE
TOPPED WITH
AMARETTO DI SARONNO

•

serves 4

THE ROSALEE STEWART B & B SALAD

Fast forward: Rosalind and Stanley are on a two-day layover in Paris picking up goodies before heading to the Ivory Coast. Guests are expected there in a few days. They will arrive after breakfast; lunch will await them, served either in the dining room or on the terrace, with a garden border of 57 varieties of flora. What's at play here is the fusion of food, which speaks of Rosalinda's Honduran background, and the Jamaican dishes that Stanley grew up on. Their roots reflect Harlem, the flavors of Africa, and their many sojourns to France. This is one of their signature salads—salmon on a bed of greens, topped with black beans, goat cheese, cherry tomatoes, and balsamic vinaigrette.

BEANS

1+1/2 cups dried black beans

2 tablespoons extra-virgin olive oil

1 medium onion, chopped

2 cloves garlic, chopped

1 teaspoon dried rosemary

1 teaspoon herbes de Provence

1 hot red pepper, seeds removed and finely minced

Salt, to taste

DRESSING

4 large cloves garlic

1/3 cup balsamic vinegar

1 teaspoon fresh lemon juice

1 teaspoon Dijon mustard

1 teaspoon honey

1/4 teaspoon dried rosemary

1/4 teaspoon herbes de Provence

1/3 cup extra-virgin olive oil

Salt and freshly ground black pepper, to taste

SALMON

4 (4-ounce) salmon fillets

2 tablespoons extra-virgin olive oil

Salt and freshly ground black pepper, to taste

6 large cloves garlic, thinly sliced

SALAD

4 cups mixed salad greens

1 cup cherry tomatoes

4 tablespoons goat cheese

Prepare the beans: Rinse the beans. Place them in a large saucepan with cold water to cover by 2 inches. Soak overnight.

Drain the beans and discard the water. Rinse the beans and cover again with cold water. Bring the beans to a boil, and lower to a simmer.

Heat the oil in a large skillet over low to medium heat, and sauté the onion and garlic until softened. Add to the simmering beans. Add the rosemary, herbes de Provence, hot pepper, and salt. Simmer over medium-high heat until the beans are tender, about 1 hour, stirring occasionally.

Meanwhile, make the dressing. Force the garlic through a garlic press and place in a small bowl. Whisk in the balsamic vinegar, lemon juice, mustard, honey, rosemary, and herbes de Provence. Add the oil in a steady stream, whisking until blended. Season with salt and pepper.

Drain the beans thoroughly. Add half the dressing to the beans, and set the beans aside.

Prepare the salmon: Brush the salmon all over with 1 tablespoon of the olive oil. In a large skillet, heat the remaining 1 tablespoon olive oil over medium-high heat. Cook the salmon, skin side down, for 6 minutes. Season with salt and pepper. Turn the salmon back over, season with salt and pepper and place the garlic slices on top. Turn the salmon over and cook for 5 minutes. Turn the salmon over and cook for 1 minute.

Divide the greens among 4 large plates, spreading the greens out and pressing them down to lay flat. Place a salmon fillet on top of each salad. Place several spoonfuls of the beans over the salmon and salad. Add the tomatoes and goat cheese and top with a spoonful of vinaigrette. Serves 4.

GOLDEN-YELLOW BANANA CORNBREAD

If that salad doesn't knock you out, just pair this cornbread with it. Now you understand what the fusion is all about.

Butter, for pan

2 very overripe bananas

1 cup yellow cornmeal, such as Indian Head brand

1 cup sifted whole-wheat flour

1/4 cup raw sugar, such as turbinado

1 tablespoon baking powder

1 teaspoon salt

1/4 cup vegetable shortening

2 eggs, beaten

3/4 cup milk

1/4 cup heavy cream

1/2 teaspoon cinnamon

1 teaspoon pure almond extract

Preheat the oven to 375°. Butter a 9-inch square baking pan. Peel the bananas, mash them in a large bowl, and set aside.

In a medium bowl, combine the cornmeal, flour, sugar, baking powder, and salt.

Add the shortening, eggs, milk, and cream to the mashed bananas and combine. Add the dry ingredients with a few swift strokes.

Add the cinnamon and almond extract to the mixture with a few more strokes. Pour the batter into the prepared pan and bake until golden and a toothpick inserted in the middle comes out clean, about 30 minutes. Serves 6 to 8.

PEAR PIE TOPPED WITH AMARETTO DI SARONNO

If you can't get to Grand-Bassam for this dessert, what you do is invite this couple for dinner at your home when they are in the States. Your hostess gift will no doubt be their famous pear pie.

CRUST

1+1/4 cups bleached all-purpose flour, plus more for dusting

8 tablespoons (1 stick) unsalted butter

1/8 teaspoon salt

3 tablespoons ice water

FILLING:

7–8 pears (2+1/2 pounds), preferably Bosc or Anjou

1 tablespoon fresh lemon juice

4 tablespoons (1/2 stick) unsalted butter

1/2 cup raw sugar, such as turbinado

3/4 cup raisins

1 teaspoon pure almond extract

1/2 teaspoon freshly grated ginger

1 teaspoon freshly ground cinnamon

1/2 teaspoon grated lemon zest

1/4 cup Amaretto di Saronno

Make the crust: Place the flour, butter, and salt in a food processor. Process for about 12 seconds. Add the ice water and pulse until the pastry begins to hold together, about 10 times. Do not let the pastry form a ball. Transfer the pastry to waxed paper and cover with another piece of waxed paper; flatten the dough into a disk. If the dough seems to be too sticky, sprinkle it with additional flour, incorporating 1 tablespoon at a time. Wrap the pastry in waxed paper. Refrigerate for at least 1 hour.

Remove the dough from the refrigerator. On a lightly floured surface, carefully roll out the dough into a 12-inch circle. Transfer the dough to a 10+1/2-inch black tin tart pan with a removable bottom. With your fingertips, carefully press the pastry into the pan and up the sides, trying not to stretch it. Trim the overhang, leaving about 1 inch extending over the rim. Tuck this overhang inside the pan, pressing gently against the side to create a sturdy, double-sided rim. If you build the pastry a bit higher than the pan, you will have fewer problems with shrinkage. Chill for at least 20 minutes.

Preheat the oven to 375°. Prick the bottom of the shell with a fork. Carefully line the shell loosely with heavy-duty aluminum foil, pressing well into the edges so that the shell will not shrink during baking. Fill with pie weights, dry rice, or dry beans, making sure to get it all the way into the edges. Bake just until the pastry begins to brown around the edges and seems firm enough to stand up by itself, about 20 minutes. Remove from the oven and remove weights and foil.

Meanwhile, make the filling: Peel and core the pears; cut each pear into 12 even wedges. Toss them in a bowl with the lemon juice to prevent discoloration.

In a large skillet, melt the butter over medium heat. Add the pears, then sprinkle in the sugar, raisins, almond extract, ginger, cinnamon, and lemon zest. Sauté, lightly stirring and shaking the pan from time to time so that the pears cook evenly. Cook until lightly browned, about 15 minutes. Add the Amaretto di Saronno. Spoon the pears into the center of the prepared pie shell, arranging them carefully. Bake until golden, about 30 minutes. Serves 6 to 8.

autumn

COD FISH LOOKIN' GOOD

"Although there is an ample supply of fresh fish in the markets of the Caribbean, as well as in those in Harlem, salted cod remains a favorite. Most Jamaican and Latino restaurants have it on their take-out menu. In keeping with the tradition of the Caribbean, yellow rice is the preferred accompaniment for this dish, plus the colors of the two dishes go so beautifully with one another."

menu

•

CARIBBEAN
COD FISH AND PEPPERS

•

YELLOW RICE

•

WATERCRESS SALAD

•

LIME PIE

•

serves 4 to 6

CARIBBEAN COD FISH AND PEPPERS

1 pound boneless, skinless bacalao (dried salt cod)

1 tablespoon fresh lemon juice

2 bay leaves

6 peppercorns

2 tablespoons vegetable oil

1/2 cup (1 stick) unsalted butter

2 medium onions, sliced into rings

1 large red bell pepper, seeded and cut into strips

1 medium yellow bell pepper, seeded and cut into strips

1 large green bell pepper, seeded and cut into strips

6 plum tomatoes, cut into wedges

3 grinds fresh black pepper

Yellow rice (see recipe page 106)

Cut the dried cod into large chunks and place in a large bowl; cover with water. Add the lemon juice. Cover the bowl with plastic wrap, and refrigerate overnight, changing the water three times. The fish will become plump and most of the salt will be removed.

Drain the fish, place it in a colander, and rinse it well. In a saucepan cover the fish with 1 quart water. Add the bay leaves and peppercorns and simmer over medium heat for 20 minutes. Place the fish back in the colander and rinse again. Flake the fish (not too finely) with your hands or a fork; set aside.

In a saucepan, heat the oil and butter over medium-low heat; add the onions and bell peppers, and sauté until soft but not limp, about 5 minutes. Add the tomatoes and black pepper and simmer for another 5 minutes. Add the fish, gently stir everything together, and continue simmering for another 10 minutes. Serve with yellow rice. Serves 4 to 6.

WATERCRESS SALAD

When planning a meal, one should consider the texture, form, and color of all of the dishes to be presented. The salad for this meal should be simple, and all one color. It should not compete with the cod dish.

3 bunches watercress

1 cup extra-virgin olive oil

1/3 cup red wine vinegar

Freshly ground black pepper, to taste

Trim off watercress stems and rinse the cress several times until free of grit. Spin dry, and place in a salad bowl. Combine the oil and vinegar and pour desired amount over watercress; toss to combine. Reserve remaining dressing for another use. Arrange on salad plates, and grind fresh pepper sparingly over each portion. Serves 4 to 6.

LIME PIE

In the Caribbean this sweet and tart dessert is known as lime pie. In Harlem and elsewhere, it is called key lime pie, so named for the small and intensely tart limes found in the Florida Keys. If you can't find key limes, common limes will do very well.

3 eggs, separated

1 cup plus 3 tablespoons sugar

3 tablespoons cornstarch

2 tablespoons all-purpose flour

1/4 teaspoon salt

2+1/4 cups boiling water

1 cup fresh lime juice

1 teaspoon grated lime zest

1 tablespoon unsalted butter

1 (9-inch) piecrust (see Single-Crust Pastry, page 25, or use frozen, store-bought crust)

Preheat the oven to 350°. Beat the egg yolks well; set the whites aside. Place 1 cup of the sugar, cornstarch, flour, and salt in the top of a double boiler over simmering water, then stir in 2+1/4 cups boiling water and cook, stirring, until the mixture thickens, about 10 minutes; remove from heat. Stir a small amount of the mixture into the egg yolks. Whisk the egg yolk mixture back into the hot mixture and cook, stirring, 2 minutes. Add the lime juice, lime zest, and butter.

Prepare and prebake the piecrust, or follow the package directions on a frozen pie shell. Pour the filling into the prebaked pie shell.

Make the meringue: Beat the reserved egg whites with an electric mixer in a medium bowl until stiff but not dry, adding the remaining 3 tablespoons sugar a little at a time. Spoon the meringue over the top of the pie and bake until the top begins to brown, about 10 minutes. Cool to room temperature and then refrigerate until chilled. Serves 8.

autumn

THANKSGIVING IN HARLEM

"In Harlem, Thanksgiving has nothing to do with the Pilgrims. It is about having something to put on the table—and some do not take this for granted. We give thanks that we are able to share with family and friends, that we are healthy and together. It is a day when we remember the ancestors. Many years ago, my cousin Dona (Marimba Ani) Richards, an anthropologist and African traditionalist, first prepared a plate of food in remembrance of our ancestors. I give thanks for Dona, because she has given us a new tradition and has shown us a way to remember with tremendous esteem those who came before us, those who gave us life."

menu

•

ROASTED JERK TURKEY
WITH CORNBREAD STUFFING AND
PICKAPEPPA PERFECT GRAVY

•

COLLARD GREENS

•

SANDRA'S ORANGE-PRALINE YAMS

•

WILD RICE

•

CRANBERRY AND APPLE CHUTNEY

•

RUM CAKE

•

suggested drink:
CHÂTEAU D'AQUERIA TAVEL 2003

•

serves 6 to 8 with leftovers

ROASTED JERK TURKEY

Golden brown and magnificent on the platter, this is the turkey they will be talking about for a long time to come.

1 (12- to 16-pound) turkey, thawed if frozen

Noel Dean's jerk seasoning (recipe follows)

2–3 tablespoons olive oil

Cornbread stuffing (recipe follows)

To jerk: The night before roasting, clean and rinse the bird, and thoroughly dry with paper towels. Rub some of the jerk seasoning inside the wishbone cavity. Loosen the skin, and rub the seasoning between the skin and meat down into the breast area as far as you can. Loosen the skin between the legs, and rub the seasoning up towards the breast area between skin and meat. Rub inside the bird, and then rub the rest of the seasoning all over the skin.

To roast: Preheat the oven to 325°. Use paper towels to wipe as much of the seasoning off as you can from the skin of the turkey and from inside; the seasoning has already done its job. Brush a light coat of olive oil all over the skin. Loosely stuff the turkey with the cornbread stuffing, including the wishbone cavity. Truss the turkey by tucking the drumstick ends under the band of skin below the cavity. Some turkeys come with a metal clamp–tuck the legs into this. The drumsticks can also be tied to the tail with kitchen string. Be sure to tuck wing tips under the back.

Place the turkey breast side up on a rack in a shallow roasting pan and cover with a loose tent of aluminum foil, pressing the foil slightly to the drumsticks. Avoid having the tent touch the breast and sides. When the turkey is two-thirds of the way done, baste, and cut the band of skin so that heat can reach the inside of the thighs. Total cooking time is 3+1/2 to 4+1/2 hours.

About 20 minutes before roasting time is up, test for doneness by gently moving the drumstick up and down; it should move easily. A meat thermometer inserted into the thigh, avoiding the bone, should read 180° when it is almost done. Baste the turkey and return to oven to finish roasting for remaining 20 minutes.

Remove the turkey to a warm platter and let it rest for at least 30 minutes before carving. Serves 6 to 8.

NOEL DEAN'S JERK SEASONING

The Arawak Indians of Jamaica shared their method of preserving meat with the Maroons, runaway slaves who were so fierce in their determination not to be enslaved that they were able to survive in Jamaica's remote Boston Bay until today. There, the Maroons still lead a traditional African life. What they have done with jerk is now famous throughout the world, and once you have had it, you too will be spreading the word. If you can cook your meat out of doors with charcoal, you will capture the true essence of jerk; if not, an oven will do, and it will still be an exciting, bold new taste.

2 onions, finely chopped

4 scallions, white and green parts, finely chopped

1/4 cup fresh lime juice

2 tablespoons white vinegar

3 Scotch bonnet peppers (or jalapeño peppers), minced

2 cloves garlic, finely minced

2 tablespoons orange juice

2 tablespoons finely minced fresh rosemary leaves

1 teaspoon ground allspice

Leaves from 4 sprigs fresh thyme, finely minced

1 teaspoon salt

1/2 teaspoon cinnamon

Process all the ingredients in a food processor or blender until the mixture becomes a smooth paste. If it is too dry, add 1 tablespoon vegetable oil. Prepare this a few days prior to cooking the turkey. Stored in the refrigerator in a tightly covered jar, it will keep for several days. Makes about 1/2 cup.

CORNBREAD STUFFING

2 tablespoons olive oil

10 ounces white mushrooms, cleaned and sliced

1 medium onion, finely chopped

3 stalks celery, finely chopped

2 cloves garlic, minced

2 cups chicken stock

1 cup water

1+1/2 cups (3 sticks) unsalted butter

21 ounces store-bought cornbread stuffing, such as Pepperidge Farm or Arnold brands

2 dashes hot sauce, such as Tabasco

2 tablespoons dried parsley

1 teaspoon poultry seasoning

Salt, to taste

Preheat the oven to 325°. Heat 1 tablespoon of the oil in a large skillet over medium-high heat. Sauté the mushrooms until juices are released. Drain, and set aside. Wipe out the skillet. Add the remaining 1 tablespoon oil to the skillet and sauté the onion, celery, and garlic until softened; remove from heat and set aside.

In an large pot, bring the chicken stock and water to a boil; lower to a simmer, and add the butter. As soon as the butter has melted, remove from the heat and add the cubed cornbread; add the sautéed vegetables, and the hot sauce, parsley, and poultry seasoning and mix thoroughly. Add salt. Put the dressing in an 11x9-inch baking pan and cover with aluminum foil. The stuffing can be prepared up to this point and refrigerated several hours prior to cooking. Bake for 30 minutes. Makes enough to stuff a 20- to 23-pound turkey.

WILD RICE

3 cups wild rice

8 cups chicken stock

Rinse the wild rice, then soak it in 6 cups of cold water for 1 hour. Drain well. Bring the chicken stock to a boil in a large saucepan. Add the rice, cover, and allow to return to a boil. Lower to a simmer and cook until tender and firm but not mushy, 45 to 60 minutes. Drain off any excess stock, then fluff with a fork and serve immediately. Serves 12.

COLLARD GREENS

Use recipe on page 24, doubling the amount of collard greens to 8 pounds. The quantities of all other ingredients stay the same. Serves 12.

MY OWN ORANGE-PRALINE YAMS

In the past several years, I have played around with the Thanksgiving menu—but play with the yams, I don't think so. My family would never allow it. My uncle Frankie and I really bonded at a Thanksgiving dinner when I served them, and I celebrated moving into a new country house by cooking them for my most cherished ones, at the first Thanksgiving meal there.

4 pounds yams (or two 40-ounce cans, drained), peeled

2/3 cup orange juice

5 tablespoons brandy

4 tablespoons (1/2 stick) unsalted butter, melted

1/3 cup firmly packed light brown sugar

1 tablespoon grated orange zest

2 teaspoons salt

1 teaspoon ground ginger

3 egg yolks

3 grinds fresh black pepper

TOPPING

1 cup chopped pecans

2/3 cup firmly packed light brown sugar

1/2 cup (1 stick) unsalted butter, melted

1 teaspoon cinnamon

Preheat the oven to 350°. Butter an 11x7-inch baking dish. If using fresh yams, in a 5-quart pot, boil the yams in water to cover until tender, 25 to 30 minutes. Drain and cool, and cut into thick slices. With an electric mixer beat the yams at medium speed until smooth, about 2 minutes. Add the orange juice, brandy, melted butter, brown sugar, orange zest, salt, ginger, egg yolks, and pepper and beat for 1 minute. Spoon into the prepared dish.

Stir the topping ingredients together thoroughly; spread evenly over the yams. Bake until golden brown and bubbly, 45 to 50 minutes. Remove from the oven and let stand 10 minutes before serving. Serves 12.

CRANBERRY AND APPLE CHUTNEY

This is the kind of dish that can make your new, recently married stepdaughter cringe. She looks at you and says "Mom, this really makes it look bad for me." Not to worry; I have been at it a long time, and I have taken the time to write it all down for you. The chutney will keep for at least two weeks in the refrigerator, so this can be prepared ahead. What is left after dinner can be served with those turkey sandwiches.

1 (12-ounce) bag fresh cranberries

2 MacIntosh apples, peeled, cored, and chopped

1 cup chopped onion

1/2 cup firmly packed dark brown sugar

1/2 cup raisins

1/4 cup apple cider vinegar

2 teaspoons freshly grated lemon zest

1/4 cup peeled minced ginger

1 teaspoon mustard seeds

1/2 teaspoon crushed hot red pepper flakes

1/8 teaspoon salt

In a heavy saucepan combine all ingredients, and simmer, stirring occasionally until all of the berries have burst, 20 to 25 minutes. Serve at room temperature. Makes 4 cups.

PICKAPEPPA PERFECT GRAVY

Pickapeppa sauce is available wherever West Indian food products are sold, in specialty shops and in large supermarkets with extensive marinade and sauce sections. You will really want to have a few bottles on hand, as it does wild things with soups, beans, and whatever your imagination tells you.

1/4 cup all-purpose flour

4 cups chicken stock, or water mixed with pan juices from roasted turkey

Salt and freshly ground black pepper, to taste

2 tablespoons Pickapeppa sauce

After lifting the turkey to the platter and leaving the crusty bits in the pan, pour off the fat and pan juices into a measuring cup. When the fat rises to the top, skim it off into another measuring cup. Measure 1/2 cup fat back into the pan, then stir 1/4 cup flour into the fat, blending together with a spoon. Cook and stir over very low heat until frothy. Remove the pan from the heat, and pour in the chicken stock, or water mixed with pan juices, scraping up the crusty bits and stirring them in. Return to the heat, season with salt and pepper, add the Pickapeppa sauce, and simmer for 5 minutes. Pour into a sauceboat and serve with the turkey. Makes about 4 cups of gravy.

RUM CAKE

Butter, for pan

All-purpose flour, for pan

1 (18.5-ounce) box yellow cake mix

1 box Jell-O lemon instant pudding and pie filling

4 eggs

1 cup mango nectar

1 cup 80-proof dark rum

1/4 cup canola oil

1/4 cup raisins

1 cup sugar

Preheat the oven to 350°. Butter and flour a 12-cup Bundt pan. Combine the cake mix, pudding mix, eggs, 1/2 cup of the mango nectar, 1/2 cup of the rum, the oil, and raisins in a large bowl, and blend well, then beat at medium speed for 2 minutes. Turn into the prepared pan. Bake until a toothpick inserted into the middle of the cake comes out clean, about 1 hour.

While the cake is baking, combine the remaining 1/2 cup nectar and sugar in a saucepan. Bring to a boil; boil for 5 minutes, stirring constantly over low heat. Remove from the stove. Stir in the remaining 1/2 cup rum.

When the cake is done, let it cool in the pan for 15 minutes, then invert it onto a platter. Prick the top and sides with a fork. Slowly and carefully spoon and brush the syrup over the warm cake. Let cool completely or refrigerate, wrapped in plastic wrap, until ready to serve.

autumn

THIS WAS HARLEM

“During the '60s and '70s there was a plethora of clublike restaurants in Harlem, all serving good food. The jukeboxes played the coolest jazz, the conversations were glib, the clientele enlightened. It was chitterlings and champagne at the Red Rooster, followed by drinks at Jock's next door, and then a little music at Count Basie's—then you'd make plans to meet the next night at Obie's. Obie made the best smothered pork chops. After much pleading and many meals, he gave up the secret, which I kept for years, written on a paper napkin.”

menu

•

OBIE'S SMOTHERED
PORK CHOPS

•

SAUTÉED POTATOES
WITH APPLES

•

SAUTÉED SWISS CHARD

•

I'M TRYING
COCONUT CUSTARD PIE

•

serves 4 to 6

OBIE'S SMOTHERED PORK CHOPS

6 center-cut, 1-inch-thick pork chops

1 teaspoon salt

1 teaspoon onion powder

1 teaspoon garlic powder

1/4 teaspoon freshly ground black pepper

1/4 teaspoon cayenne pepper

1/4 cup pancake mix (the "just-add-water" kind)

2 tablespoons corn oil

GRAVY

3 medium onions, sliced

1 teaspoon salt

1/4 teaspoon freshly ground black pepper

1 tablespoon sugar

1/4 cup all-purpose flour

2 cups boiling water

Preheat the oven to 350°. Rinse the pork chops and pat dry with paper towels. Sprinkle them with the salt, onion powder, garlic powder, pepper, and cayenne pepper; coat with the pancake mix.

Heat the oil in a large skillet over medium heat; brown the chops well on both sides. Remove from the skillet to a shallow roasting pan.

Make the gravy: In the skillet you cooked the chops in, sauté the onions with the salt, pepper, and sugar until lightly browned.

Stir in the flour and cook until well blended. Gradually add the boiling water, stirring constantly, until the gravy thickens and comes to a boil. Pour over the chops in the baking pan. Cover the top of the pan tightly with aluminum foil.

Bake until golden brown and tender, about 1 hour and 20 minutes. Remove the chops to serving platter. Strain the gravy through a sieve, pressing the onions through with a wooden spoon. Skim the fat off the gravy, and serve in a gravy boat. Serves 4 to 6.

SAUTÉED POTATOES WITH APPLES

Potato lovers, listen up! If you haven't paired apples with potatoes, you are missing something. One day it was raining, and there were a few potatoes in the house and a couple of apples—not enough to make potatoes for dinner, and not enough apples to make applesauce for the pork chops, so they got a thing going on together.

2 pounds white potatoes, peeled

4 tablespoons (1/2 stick) unsalted butter

3 tablespoons corn oil

4 scallions, white and some pale green parts, chopped

2 small Granny Smith apples, peeled, cored, and cut into 1-inch cubes

1 teaspoon salt

1/4 teaspoon freshly ground black pepper

Fill a large saucepan with cold water, and place the potatoes in the water as they are peeled. When all are added, bring to a boil over high heat; boil for 15 minutes. Drain the water off, remove the potatoes from the pot, let cool, and then cut into 2-inch pieces. Set aside.

In a large skillet over low heat, combine the butter and oil. When the butter has melted, add the potatoes and scallions and sauté until golden brown, about 8 minutes. Use a spatula to scrape up the brown bits frequently as the potatoes are cooking. Add the apples, cover, and cook, shaking the pan frequently to prevent burning, 2 minutes. Remove the cover and stir, scraping the brown bits from the bottom. Continue cooking, uncovered, until the potatoes and apples are tender, about 5 minutes. Add salt and pepper. Serves 4 to 6.

SAUTÉED SWISS CHARD

Marisa Gherardi, my good neighbor in the country, is a weekend gardener. I had not heard of Swiss chard until she bestowed some on me. She suggested that I just sauté it with some garlic, which I did. I loved it. Harlem is not known for Swiss chard, but you better believe it knows about it now. It is even available at Harlem's Fairway. Do you think Marisa will give me more?

2 tablespoons extra-virgin olive oil

2 cloves fresh garlic, cut into thin slivers

3 bunches Swiss chard, rinsed several times, stems removed, leaves coarsely chopped

Heat the oil in a skillet over medium heat. Add the garlic and sauté until just golden. Add the Swiss chard and sauté, stirring, until soft, 5 to 8 minutes. Serves 4 to 6.

I'M TRYING COCONUT CUSTARD PIE

A real Harlemite is someone who has been around for a long time, and they haven't been if they can't tell you about Georgie's Bakery. This is where you stood on line to get those melt-in-your-mouth doughnuts, the kind you polished off in the car on your way home and had to turn around and get back on line for, because you dared not show up without them. Then there were the rolls and the pies, the coconut pies. . . . Like all good things, it all came to an end when the bakery closed. After 40 years in business, they decided that it was time to retire. So now we make our own pies and rolls, and hope they turn out as well.

3 egg yolks

1/2 cup sugar

1 tablespoon cornstarch

1/2 cup milk

3/4 cup shredded sweetened coconut

1 tablespoon butter, cut into small pieces

2 tablespoons rum

1 prebaked 9-inch piecrust (use Single-Crust Pastry, page 25, or a store-bought frozen pie shell, thawed)

Beat the egg yolks and sugar until thick and light; stir in the cornstarch. Scald the milk and stir a little into the egg yolk mixture; add this back into the hot milk. Bring the mixture to a boil, stirring constantly, and cook until thick and shiny, about 1 minute. Stir in the coconut and cook 1 minute longer. Remove the pan from the heat, beat in the butter, a small piece at a time, and stir in the rum. Pour filling into the prebaked pie shell and let cool, cover completely with plastic when cooled, and refrigerate. Serves 6.

"POOL HALL"

autumn

WHAT THE MEN COOK FOR BREAKFAST

“Everyone in Harlem has their favorite fish-and-chips joint. You don't have to go far to find one. The fish is usually whiting, sometimes porgies. Some places bread the fish, others flour it, so depending on how you like it, that's where you go. When fried fish turns up at Kevin Edwards's house for breakfast, it starts your day off on the right track, especially when brother-in-law Tony Carter finishes the meal off with moonshine margaritas. Kenny Vaughn works the potatoes, and Twan Evans the corn muffins. It's a guy thing.”

menu

•

KEVIN'S FISH FRY

•

KENNY'S
HOME-FRIED POTATOES

•

TWAN'S JALAPEÑO
CORN MUFFINS

•

serves 4 to 6

KEVIN'S FISH FRY

1 large red bell pepper, thinly sliced into rings

1 medium onion, cut in half lengthwise then thinly sliced crosswise

1 cup cornmeal

1 teaspoon salt

1/2 teaspoon freshly ground black pepper

1/2 teaspoon onion powder

1/4 teaspoon cayenne pepper

3 pounds whiting fillets, cut in half lengthwise

1/4 cup corn oil or canola oil

Preheat the oven to 175°. Place half of the red pepper and onion slices in a large paper bag; set aside. In a small bowl, mix the cornmeal with salt, black pepper, onion powder and cayenne pepper. Place the cornmeal mix in a large plastic food storage bag. Add the fish to the cornmeal, a few pieces at a time. Shake to coat.

Pour the oil into a large, heavy skillet over medium heat. When the oil is hot, add half of the fish. Fry until golden brown, 3+1/2 to 5 minutes, turning over occasionally. With a slotted spoon, remove the fish from the skillet; place immediately in the paper bag with the peppers and onions. Hold the bag closed. Shake gently and remove the fish and vegetables, placing them in a paper-towel–lined baking dish. Place in warm oven until ready to serve. Repeat steps with the second batch of fish and remaining peppers and onions, adding more oil to skillet if needed. Serves 6.

KENNY'S HOME-FRIED POTATOES

2 pounds white potatoes, peeled

1/3 cup corn oil or bacon drippings

3/4 cup diced green bell pepper

1 large onion, chopped into 1-inch dice

1 teaspoon paprika

Salt and freshly ground black pepper, to taste

Place the potatoes in a large saucepan with cold water to cover. Bring to a boil, and lower heat; simmer on medium-high for 15 minutes. When cool enough to handle cut into 1-inch cubes.

Warm the oil in a 10-inch skillet over medium heat; add the potatoes, green pepper, and onion. Sprinkle the paprika over the potatoes, add salt, and a good amount of freshly ground pepper. Sauté until the potatoes are golden and the pepper and onion are soft, about 10 minutes; turn occasionally to brown all sides, and scrape up the bottom of the pan as you turn them. Serves 6.

TWAN'S JALAPEÑO CORN MUFFINS

Twan's dad isn't invited to this breakfast as the stories may be too colorful. Young men like to hold forth about their "conquests," in the same way fisherman talk about the one that didn't get away. Twan still saves a muffin for his dad, to prove that he can "burn," that is, really cook, too.

1/3 cup (5+1/3 tablespoons) butter, melted

1 cup stone-ground yellow cornmeal

1 cup all-purpose flour

2 tablespoons sugar

1 tablespoon baking powder

3/4 teaspoon salt

3 large eggs

1 cup milk

3 fresh or pickled jalapeño peppers, seeded and finely chopped

Preheat the oven to 400°. Use 1 tablespoon of the butter to grease a 12-cup muffin tin. In a medium bowl whisk together the cornmeal, flour, sugar, baking powder, and salt. In another bowl mix together the remaining butter, the eggs, milk, and jalapeños. Add to the cornmeal mixture, stirring just until combined. Do not overbeat. Spoon the batter into the greased muffin pan, leaving 1/4 inch unfilled at the top. Bake until the tops are golden brown and a toothpick inserted into the center comes out clean, about 30 minutes. Makes 12 muffins.

INDEX

D

E

LIST OF ILLUSTRATIONS BY BENNY ANDREWS

Intro: *The Cotton Club (Migrant Series)*, 2004. Oil and collage on canvas.

pg 31: *Sunday*, 1994. Oil and collage on canvas, High Museum of Art.

pg 69: *Apollo (Langston Hughes Series)*, 1996. Oil and collage on paper.

pg 75: *New Arrival (Migrant Series)*, 2004. Oil and collage on paper.

pg 81: *New Arrival (Langston Hughes Series)*, 1996. Oil and collage on paper, private collection.

pg 127: *Harlem USA (Migrant Series)*, 2004. Oil and collage on paper.
Illustration by Benny Andrews used with permission of Sterling Publishing Co., Inc., NY, NY from POETRY FOR YOUNG PEOPLE: LANGSTON HUGHES, edited by David Roessel & Arnold Rampersad, artwork © 2006 by Benny Andrews.

pg 139: *Blues Over Harlem (Musical Interlude Series)*, 1998. Oil and collage on paper.

pg 157: *Blue Lady (Music Series)*, 1995. Oil and collage on paper, private collection.

pg 181: *Pool Hall*, 1985. Oil and collage on paper.

A POSTHUMOUS ACKNOWLEDGMENT

The family of Sandra Lawrence wishes to thank Hiroko Kiiffner and Lake Isle Press for their patience and support during Sandra's long illness. We are sincerely grateful for your decision to continue with publication of *Harlem Really Cooks* after her passing. You have given us a most meaningful way of cherishing her memory.